Carmack's
Guide to
Copyright & Contracts

BOOKS BY
SHARON DEBARTOLO CARMACK

GENEALOGICAL GUIDEBOOKS
The Family Tree Guide to Finding Your Ellis Island Ancestors
You Can Write Your Family History
Your Guide to Cemetery Research
A Genealogist's Guide to Discovering Your Immigrant and Ethnic Ancestors
Organizing Your Family History Search
A Genealogist's Guide to Discovering Your Female Ancestors
The Genealogy Sourcebook
Italian-American Family History: A Guide to Researching and Writing About Your Heritage

FAMILY HISTORY NARRATIVES/COMPILED GENEALOGIES
Italians in Transition: The Vallarelli Family of Terlizzi, Italy, and Westchester County, New York and The DeBartolo Family of Terlizzi, Italy, New York, and San Francisco, California
A Sense of Duty: The Life and Times of Jay Roscoe Rhoads and his wife, Mary Grace Rudolph
My Wild Irish Rose: The Life of Rose (Norris) (O'Connor) Fitzhugh and her mother Delia (Gordon) Norris
David and Charlotte Hawes (Buckner) Stuart of King George County, Virginia, Including Three Generations of Their Descendants
American Lives and Lines, co-authored with Roger D. Joslyn
The Ebetino and Vallarelli Family History: Italian Immigrants to Westchester County, New York

PUBLISHED ABSTRACTS AND REFERENCE GUIDES
Communities at Rest: An Inventory and Field Study of Five Eastern Colorado Cemeteries
The Family Tree Resource Book for Genealogists, co-editor with Erin Nevius

Carmack's Guide to Copyright & Contracts

A Primer for Genealogists, Writers & Researchers

Sharon DeBartolo Carmack, CG

Foreword by
Karen Kreider Gaunt, Attorney at Law

Published by Genealogical Publishing Co., Inc.
Baltimore, Maryland
www.genealogical.com
Library of Congress Catalogue Card Number 2005924569
International Standard Book Number 0-8063-1758-2
Made in the United States of America

Disclaimer

This book is not intended as legal advice. Because the law is dynamic and not always black and white, neither the author nor the publisher can assume responsibility for any actions taken based on information contained in this book. This book is meant to be informational and to give genealogists and writers an awareness of copyright, fair use, the public domain, and publishing contracts. When in doubt about any issue relating to copyright, seek legal advice from an experienced intellectual property or publishing law attorney.

Contents

Acknowledgments

This book, like most others, was years in the making. While I had always had an interest in copyright issues, it wasn't until 1999 that I had a baptism by fire in the topic. At the end of that year, my colleague Roger D. Joslyn and I found ourselves defending our copyright in a federal court of law. I immediately turned for help to intellectual property attorney Karen Kreider Gaunt, a partner at the law firm of Keating, Muething & Klekamp, PLL, in Cincinnati, Ohio. A year or so earlier, Karen had helped me negotiate a book contract, and at the time, she was with another law firm. Ironically, that firm, which had offices in another part of the country, represented in a separate case the same client who was suing us, so Karen couldn't represent us. After she moved to Keating, Muething & Klekamp, she was able to represent us as the copyright consultant on our case. Since the settlement of that suit, Karen has continued to represent me and answer any of my copyright questions, and she helped me to resolve an infringement of my copyright when someone, without my permission, videotaped one of my lectures at a national conference. So I want to extend my gratitude to her for being my attorney and for generously making time to review this manuscript and write the foreword.

Also representing us in our lawsuit were New York attorneys and litigators George Hinckley and Louis Lustenberger. I wish to thank them not only for handling our case, but also for all they taught us about the legal system and intellectual property.

Roger, of course, agreed to let me tell our lawsuit story, initially in the *Association of Professional Genealogists Quarterly*, and then again in this book. Thanks, Rog.

I suppose, in some way, I should thank the client who sued us. While it was a tumultuous and stressful time, how many people can say they've been sued in federal court? And what unexpected bonuses we got: We've left a new record of ourselves for our descendants to find! Even though the lawsuit was costly, we also got quite an education. (Then again, where can you get that kind of education for free?)

Another colleague gave her consent to reprint an article we wrote for *Writer's Digest* magazine. Appreciation goes to Maureen A. Taylor, author of several books on photographs, for not only letting me use our article here, but for reviewing the chapter on illustrations and photographs.

All writers need editors. I'm grateful to Brad Crawford for copyediting the manuscript, and to Erin Nevius for proofreading the final pages. Both are not only colleagues, but have become friends as well. It's hard to imagine writing a book without their talent and expertise working behind the scenes.

It's the custom in writing a book to thank those closest to you last. I'm not sure why that is, but why break from tradition now? James W. Warren, my partner in so many ways, read the manuscript, offered comments, provided additional questions, and proofed the index. For that, for his love, patience, and support, and for becoming a cat person, I'm grateful beyond words.

And finally, I'm supposed to say here that any remaining errors are my responsibility. I'm not sure why that is either, since that was the point of having several people read this over to make sure I hadn't made any mistakes. Shouldn't it be their responsibility? Alas, I'm afraid it's mine. But if you have any questions, feel free to talk to my attorney.

Foreword

Copyright law often is a legal maze, full of seemingly counter-intuitive, illogical, and often complicated schemes. It dictates, among other things, such basic issues as what is protected by copyright, who owns what rights, how long those rights last, how copyright ownership and rights are conveyed and transferred, and how one can use others' creative works within the parameters of the law. There are relatively few "black-and-white" answers to copyright questions. Navigating the Copyright Act and its various changes, amendments, and revisions can confuse even lawyers and practitioners who don't regularly practice in the field.

For authors, photographers, researchers, and genealogists who are creating books, articles, studies, and client reports, understanding what is protected by copyright; what rights vest in the author upon creation of any expressive work; how these rights can be licensed, conveyed, assigned, or transferred; when and how to register copyrights; and how best to negotiate the rights and obligations that come with creating such works can be a daunting task. Numerous misconceptions surround even basic issues, such as work for hire, fair use, public domain, and publication. An author or genealogist operating under one of these misconceptions could find herself faced with serious misunderstandings, loss of business and clients, harm to reputation and goodwill, and, at worst, litigation in federal court.

Complicating matters is the fact that most clients commissioning specific works—the very type of project in which most genealogists will be engaged—mistakenly believe that because they have commissioned and/or paid for the work, they own it. Many laypersons also misunderstand the difference between owning or possessing a physical manuscript and owning the copyright, as well as the panoply of rights protected under copyright's "bundle of rights."

Surprisingly, while many authors and genealogists have indepth conversations with their clients about the intended finished work and negotiate printing costs, travel fees, and other out-of-pocket expenses, they often don't discuss the ultimate question of who owns the copyright and how the work will be used and distributed. At minimum, this can lead to unpleasantness for all involved. Even though the author is the owner of the work with the right to control reproductions, publications, and distribution, most clients have entirely different expectations and won't be pleased when they eventually learn the realities of copyright law.

Another pitfall authors and researchers face when creating expressive works involves use of third-party materials. What is protected by copyright? What is in the public domain? How do I know whether I can use materials I found in public resources or on the Internet? What are the boundaries of fair use? How much can I quote from someone else's work? When am I required to get permissions from third parties?

In addition, if a work is to be published as a book or journal, often it is up to authors to review and negotiate publishing contracts for their work. This too can raise a host of issues that, if not fully understood, can leave authors with publishing contracts that are unreasonable, or at least less than satisfactory.

Although there are a myriad of issues involved in copyright law, you don't need an attorney to answer many of the basic questions. At last, a work has come along that skillfully navigates these issues and more with straightforward, easy-to-read explanations in a question-and-answer format. *Carmack's Guide to Copyright & Contracts: A Primer for Genealogists, Writers & Researchers* demystifies this subject and provides practical, real-world advice to authors, researchers, and genealogists everywhere.

Well-researched and thorough, *Carmack's Guide to Copyright & Contracts* covers everything from the who, what, and where of copyright law to strategies for determining whether something is in the public domain. It also provides excellent summaries of the often-misunderstood work-for-hire and fair use doctrines and clear, step-by-step advice to understanding, reviewing, and instituting "best practices" when negotiating book, journal, and electronic publishing contracts.

Sharon DeBartolo Carmack delivers valuable insights into the genealogist/client relationship and spotlights common pitfalls. Drawing on her experience as a researcher, genealogist, author, lecturer, and unfortunate court defendant, she guides readers on how to ensure that their intellectual property rights are protected and to likewise explain to their clients the process and their rights and obligations.

With this guide at hand, authors, researchers, and genealogists will have the knowledge necessary to develop genealogical projects to their fullest potential and for all parties to collaborate with shared expectations, goals, and desires. Their professional libraries aren't complete without it.

—Karen Kreider Gaunt
Keating, Muething & Klekamp, P.L.L.
Cincinnati, Ohio

Introduction

All you wanted to do was trace your ancestors and learn about your family history. You never realized that, in order to pursue your heritage successfully, you'd have to become a student of history, sociology, customs, traditions, historical laws, and geography. And now there's a new realm you need to learn about: copyright.

All genealogists need to know some basics of copyright law because of the nature of our pursuit. When we embark on the journey to find our ancestors, we realize that we aren't the only person descended from a forebear. Depending on how long ago the ancestor lived, that person could have thousands of descendants. Not everyone will be interested in the family history, of course, but for those who are, we find ourselves sharing information we've uncovered in exchange for our cousins sharing with us.

WHY YOU NEED THIS BOOK

What happens if a cousin takes something you've researched and claims it as her own, or she posts it to her Web site without your permission? Genealogists usually have no problem sharing, but they're rather territorial and with good reason. If you've spent twenty years researching something and made the breakthrough, you want and should receive credit for that. So what are your rights to that discovery? What do you do if someone has infringed on your copyright?

1

You may want to put your research on the Internet, and you know you should include the copyright symbol, but do you have to register with the Copyright Office? How do you do so when your research is online?

You may want to write a book for a genealogical publisher, and the contract is far more in-depth than you imagined. Should you hire a lawyer to review it and look out for your interests?

You may want to write an article for a genealogical publication, but you've been asked to sign a contract. You don't understand all the language, what rights you have, and what rights you're being asked to assign to the publisher. Later, you may want to use what you've written in your family history. Can you do so without the publisher's permission?

You've written a report or family history for a client. The client claims he owns the copyright because he commissioned the work. Is that correct? Or does the researcher own the client report? What does "work for hire" really mean under copyright law? Are you free to use the report for certification purposes without the client's permission? Can you take an excerpt of the client's family history and write an article without permission?

You may want to reprint an illustration or some text from someone else's work. Do you need to ask permission? When is it considered "fair use"?

You have a family photograph you want to use in your book or on your Web site. Do you need to get the family member's permission? What about the photographer's permission?

You want to publish an ancestor's diary. Do you need permission from all the heirs to do so? And what if the original diary is held by a repository? Does it own the copyright, and do you need its permission?

You've no doubt heard that there are works in the public domain that you can use freely without permission. Is everything on the Internet in the public domain? How do you find works in the public domain?

Perhaps you're a genealogical lecturer or teacher. Is your lesson and lecture protected by copyright? Can a student or audience member tape your lecture without your permission? Or, suppose you want to photocopy an article and distribute it to your class. Do you need permission to do that? And whose permission do you ask: the author's, editor's, or publisher's?

Clearly, genealogists have a lot of copyright concerns. While this book is not meant as legal advice or the be-all, end-all on copyright issues, it is meant to inform and educate you on the fundamentals of copyright as it pertains to your genealogical endeavors. With this book, I want you to learn enough about copyright so that you know your rights, when to seek permission, how to avoid infringing on another's copyright, and where to turn for more information.

WHY I WROTE THIS BOOK

I am not an intellectual property attorney or any other kind of attorney or paralegal. I'm a fellow genealogist and writer who has had the same questions you do. Even though this guide has been reviewed by an intellectual property attorney and is meant to enlighten you on copyright and publishing issues, it is not intended as legal advice. Anyone who has tried to understand the law knows that nothing is black and white. That's why we have lawyers. If you have questions, you should consult with an intellectual property attorney.

So why am I writing this book? Clearly there's a need for a guide written in plain English for genealogists and genealogical writers that deals with the issues we face on a day-to-day basis. Although I'm not an attorney or a paralegal, I've had training in copyright issues and publishing agreements. I've been a contract advisor for the National Writers Union since early 2001, where I've undergone formal training in copyright and publishing contracts. When authors are offered a contract, as union members, they are entitled to free contract advice from the Contract Advice Division. Most of us are not attorneys. We're fellow writers who've "been there, done that" and have attended union-sponsored classes and seminars on copyright and contracts in order to become contract advisors.

As the executive editor of Family Tree Books (formerly Betterway Genealogy Books), I've had to answer writers' questions about copyright. Often these were the same questions I've had as a writer.

But perhaps my most unusual training came when a colleague, Roger D. Joslyn, and I were sued in federal court over a copyright dispute in 1999, which you'll read more about in chapter four. We had written a family history for a client who claimed he was the copyright owner. We claimed we owned the copyright. Consequently, the client sued us in federal court, since copyright is governed exclusively by federal law. During our lawsuit, I did much independent study on copyright laws and learned quite a bit from my attorneys. So I guess you could say my training in copyright and publishing agreements has also come from the School of Hard Knocks.

Perhaps the biggest advantage of my not being a lawyer is I'm able to cut out the legal mumbo-jumbo and get to the issues and topics of concern to genealogists in language the average person can understand. In each chapter, I'll give an overview of the topic, then deal with specific scenarios genealogists encounter. This book is meant solely as a primer on U.S. copyright laws and publishing contracts. It's not meant as a replacement for consulting with an intellectual property or publishing law attorney, and I won't be covering trademarks, service marks, or patents.

It's also important to remember that copyright laws change. For changes and additions to copyright laws after the publication of this book and until a revised edition is in print, consult the Copyright Office Web site <www.copyright.gov>, where you'll also find helpful circulars, forms for filing copyright, and an extensive list of frequently asked questions. While this book covers only U.S. copyright law, in the bibliography, I've listed Internet sources to learn more about copyright laws abroad, which vary from American laws. So let's begin!

Chapter 1
Copyright Basics

Copyright is a federal law that dates back to the writing of the U.S. Constitution in 1787, which states "the Congress shall have power ... to promote the progress of science and useful arts, by securing for limited times to authors and inventors the exclusive right to their respective writings and discoveries" (Article I, Section 8, Clause 8). James Madison (whom I'm happy to claim as a relative) is the person who suggested there should be a provision of the Constitution "to secure to literary authors their copyrights for a limited time." The first Copyright Act took effect on 31 May 1790, when the term of copyright was fourteen years with the privilege to renew it for another fourteen. Since the 1790s, the copyright laws have been revised and modified as needs have changed and issues have arisen.

According to Stephen Fishman in *The Copyright Handbook* (2/2), copyright is a "legal device that provides the creator of a work of art or literature, or a work that conveys information or ideas, the right to control how the work is used." Copyright is needed to promote the progress of the arts and sciences. After all, how many people would bother creating something if, as soon as they put it out to the public, another person could claim it as his or her own? Therefore, Fishman continues, "Copyright encourages authors in their creative efforts by giving them a mini-monopoly over their works."

Copyright consists of a bundle of rights, such as the right to make and distribute copies of a work, the right to create adaptations or derivative works, and the right to perform or display the work. But only the copyright holder—the author or creator—may exercise these rights, unless the author has transferred or licensed them to another party. (See chapter six.) If someone wrongfully uses the material, the copyright owner can sue and seek compensation for any losses.

Copyright is one type of intangible rights called "intellectual property." Like any property you own, you can do whatever you want with it. Let's liken it to a piece of real property. If you own your house and the property on which it stands, you can do whatever you want with it. You can keep it all. You can sell pieces of it. You can rent the entire thing or just selected rooms in the house. You can sell it all, in which case, you have no further claim on that house or property. The same is true of copyright. After you write an article, lecture, client report, or a family history, you are automatically the copyright holder the minute you put it in a fixed or tangible form. A fixed or tangible form can be a printed manuscript, published on the Web, digitized on a CD or DVD, printed on paper, or audio- or videotaped, to name a few.

A work doesn't have to be published to be protected by copyright, but there is a distinction between works that are published and unpublished in terms of how long copyright lasts, which you'll read about later. The Copyright Law says that "publication is the distribution of copies ... of a work to the public...." If you distribute copies of your work to the public, such as to relatives, to libraries, for sale, on loan, to share, or by subscription, then you have published your work. Posting your work to the Internet is considered publication. A lecture would not be considered published unless it was audio- or videotaped and made available to the public; however, your written lecture would be protected as an unpublished work.

As the copyright holder to the work, you can grant or license different rights out of your bundle of rights to different people. For example, let's say you wrote a book. You can grant the right to publish it as a print book to Publisher A. You can grant the right to publish it on a CD-ROM to Publisher B. You can grant the right to publish an excerpt of your book in a magazine to Publisher C. And you can grant the right to publish it in a foreign language to Publisher D. As long as you have not relinquished any of these specific rights to any one person or entity, you are free to do with the material whatever you wish with the rights you still hold.

WHAT'S PROTECTED BY COPYRIGHT?

Works must be "original" to qualify for copyright protection. Originality means that a work wasn't copied from a preexisting work. There can be several books on Irish genealogical research, for example, but each would be considered original as long as one wasn't copied from another.

Here are the types of works that would be protected by copyright:

- Written materials: books, magazines, newspapers, diaries, manuscripts, letters, e-mails, poetry, catalogs, brochures, ads, directories, encyclopedias, electronic databases, computer programs, term papers, text on Web pages
- Pictorial, graphic, and sculptural works: photographs, prints, art reproductions, maps, charts, cartoons and cartoon characters, drawings, paintings, diagrams, statues, dolls, logo designs, Web page designs
- Motion pictures and other audiovisual works, including interactive multimedia works, home movies and videos

- Musical works
- Dramatic works
- Pantomime and choreographic works
- Sound recordings
- Architectural works

Copyright does not protect these items:

- Works in the public domain (see chapter two)
- Ideas, concepts, procedures, principles (Your creative expression of ideas, concepts, procedures, and principles in a fixed and tangible form is protected; the ideas, concepts, procedures, and principles themselves can't be protected.)
- Facts, information, and research data (Your creative expression of facts, information, and research data put in a fixed and tangible form is protected; the underlying facts, information, and research data themselves can't be protected.)
- Names, slogans, and titles of books, lectures, stories, articles, poems, songs, movies, etc. (These might be protected by trademark. Using someone's title or slogan would be unethical. It also could be protected by law and considered "unfair competition" if that title or slogan becomes associated in the public's mind with a particular person. See pages 17–18.)
- Blank forms designed solely to record information but that do not convey information (Blank family group sheets and pedigree charts would not be protected by copyright, but their creative design can be protected.)
- Recipes (The instructions might be protected, but the list of ingredients can't be.)
- Extemporaneous speeches (An off-the-cuff lesson or lecture isn't protected, unless it was recorded in order to meet the "fixed" requirement. See page 7.).

- U.S. federal government works (Some state and local government documents might be protected by copyright.)
- Literary plots, themes, and settings
- Calendars, measuring devices, and height and weight charts

COPYRIGHT DURATION

Copyright does not last forever. If a work was created on or after 1 January 1978, copyright protection lasts for the life of the author plus seventy years. If a work was created before 1 January 1978, but it was published between then and the end of 2002, it's protected for the life of the author plus seventy years or until the end of 2047, whichever is greater. Any work published or created before 1923 is now in the public domain (covered more in chapter two). If a work was published between 1923 and 1978, different rules apply. Confused? On pages 11 and 12, there is a simplified chart, but exceptions still apply. For more details, see the chart at <www.unc.edu/~unclng/public-d.htm>, "When Works Pass into the Public Domain," or refer to chapter three of the U.S. Copyright Law, "Duration of Copyright," which is available online at <www.copyright.gov/title17/92chap3.html>. Also see "New Rules for Using Public Domain Materials," by Lloyd J. Jassin at <www.copylaw.com/new_articles/PublicDomain.html>, information at AuthorsLawyer.com at <www.authorslawyer.com/c-term.shtml>, and Lee Wilson's *The Copyright Guide*.

Remember, there are exceptions to the chart on pages 11–12. For example, anonymous or pseudonymous works and works for hire (see chapter four) created in or after 1978 (or created but not published or registered before 1978) are protected for shorter terms: ninety-five years from the date of publication or 120 years from the year of creation. Different terms also apply to a corporation (such as a publisher) who holds the copyright. If more than one author is involved, copyright lasts for the life of the longest-living author plus seventy years. Obviously, copyright is not black and white. There are many gray areas and changes with each revision of the law, so when in doubt, seek the advice of an intellectual property attorney.

Under the present law, copyright terms expire at the end of a calendar year. So regardless of when a work was created during a given year, it won't expire until the end of the seventieth year after the author's death. For example, if the author died in April 2008, the copyright would expire on 31 December 2078.

Date of Work	Term of Copyright
Published before 1923	Copyright has expired; the work is now in the public domain and cannot be retroactively protected.
Published from 1923–1963	28 years; it could be renewed for 47 years, which has now been extended another 20 years for a total renewal of 67 years, for a maximum protection of 95 years. If not renewed during its 28th year, then copyright has expired and the work is in the public domain. Works published in 1923 with the proper copyright notice won't enter the public domain until 1 January 2019. A work published in, say, 1930, assuming it was properly renewed, won't go into the public domain until the end of 2025. If the work was published without the proper copyright notice, the work went into the public domain upon publication.
Published from 1964–1977	28 years for first term, with an automatic renewal of 67 years for the second term. If the work was published without the proper copyright notice, the work went into the public domain upon publication.
Created before 1 January 1978 and published between then and 31 December 2002	Life plus 70 or until 31 December 2047, whichever is greater.

Created before 1 January 1978 but not published	Life plus 70 years or 31 December 2002, whichever is greater. Unpublished works by an author who died before 1935 are now in the public domain.
Created on or after 1 January 1978, whether published or not	Life plus 70 years.

REGISTERING YOUR WORK

In 1870, the Copyright Office in Washington, DC, was established to oversee the registration of creative works. (Prior to that time, claims were filed with the clerks of U.S. District Courts.) While it's not necessary for you to register your work for it to be protected, you're making a public record of your claim. A copyright registration is required to bring a copyright infringement suit and/or to defend or counterclaim on the basis that you own the copyright. At a minimum, an application should be filed prior to instituting a copyright action or defending a lawsuit on the basis of copyright ownership. Another benefit is that if you own the registration prior to the act of infringement, you're entitled to statutory damages provided for in the copyright act (up to $150,000, if the infringement is shown to be willful). You can opt for statutory damages in lieu of having to prove your actual damages. You also may be entitled to attorney's fees if your work is registered prior to the infringement. Finally, registration means a copy of your work automatically will be donated to the Library of Congress.

Registering your work is not difficult. You'll find complete instructions and different forms for each type of work online at the Copyright Office Web site <www.copyright.gov/register/>. There is also a software package for purchase, making the process even easier: Official Copyright <www.officialsoftware.com>.

You'll need to send the Copyright Office two copies of your work, the required form, and the current fee. (As of this writing, it is $30 for a published work.) You'll receive a certificate of registration, but it generally takes about four to five months to process. To ensure that the Copyright Office received your application, send it with a return receipt from the post office. If your application is incomplete, you'll receive a letter from the Copyright Office asking for additional information.

Although it isn't a requirement to include the copyright notice for it to be protected, it is in your best interest to do so. Copyright Law §401, Notice of Copyright, says, "If a notice appears on the copies, it shall consist of the following three elements:

(1) the symbol © ...
(2) the year of first publication of the work ...
(3) the name of the owner[s] of copyright in the work...."

Thus, a copyright notice would look like this:

© 2005 Your Name Here

APPLYING IT TO GENEALOGY
Note: For questions on electronic issues not covered here, see chapter eight.

Can I reprint several pages from a family history published in 1896?

You don't need anyone's permission to reprint information from a family history that was published in 1896. In fact, you could reprint the entire book without permission if you wanted. The work is in the public domain. It was published prior to 1923, and therefore, the copyright has expired. For more on the public domain, see chapter two.

I want to reprint my grandmother's obituary. Do I need permission?

It depends on when the obituary was published. If she died prior to 1923 and the obituary was published prior to that date, you won't need permission. If the obituary was published after 1923, refer to the chart on pages 11–12. Then see chapter two for how to seek permission.

Let's say that, in compiling your family history for publication, you found an obituary for your grandmother who died in 1979. You either want to reproduce the entire obituary or transcribe it verbatim. Under the copyright law, any work created after 1 January 1978 is protected for the life of the author plus seventy years. But it's an obituary in a newspaper, and you don't have a clue who the author is. It could have been a family member or the newspaper staff.

If a newspaper staff person wrote the obituary, by virtue of being an employee of that newspaper, by law, under the work for hire doctrine, the newspaper, as the employer, would own the copyright. (For more on work for hire, see chapter four.) While the facts in the obituary are not protected, the creative expression part is, even if it appears to be "formula" writing. Technically, you need written permission from the newspaper publisher who holds the copyright to reproduce or fully transcribe that obituary.

Will the newspaper publisher sue you if it happens upon your family history and sees the obituary? Although the publisher is within its rights to file a lawsuit, chances are it won't, unless your grandmother happened to be a high-profile, famous individual and the obituary contains more than what a normal obituary would contain. Typically, obituaries don't carry a lot of economic value and wouldn't be worth the money and time to sue you.

If the obituary was written by a family member, and you don't know who wrote it, the odds are the same if the person discovered you reprinted it without permission: It wouldn't be worth the person's time or money to sue you for reprinting it.

Can I publish my great-grandfather's diary written in 1895?

A work created before 1978 but never published is protected for the life of the author plus 70 years or until 31 December 2002, whichever is greater. The question now becomes, when did Great-grandpa die? Let's say he died in 1939. The work is still protected. It's protected for his life plus seventy years. So that would be until the end of 2009.

Unless the diary is assigned to you in a will, the copyright on the diary belongs to all of your great-grandfather's heirs. If by will or inheritance you are the heir to the diary, then you can do with it whatever you choose. Just because you physically possess the diary, however, does not mean that you own the copyright.

Can I publish my ancestor's Civil War diary and letters he wrote to his wife while he was gone?

Genealogist Ann Lainhart wanted to publish the Civil War letters and diaries of the Bryant-Stephens families. These documents had not been published before, and this was before the copyright had expired on them at the end of 2002, putting them in the public domain. A lawyer told her that in most cases a publication of Civil War letters and diaries generates little income for the author/editor, so most people don't worry about securing all the descendants' permissions. But Ann felt it best to get everyone's permission to remove any future problems. She sought the permission of twenty-seven descendants, all of whom relinquished their copyright. "It was a pain," Lainhart said, "but I felt that after the fourteen years I put into this project and the ten years my fellow editors each put into it, that we were entitled to the royalties or anything else that happened." The book, *Rose Cottage Chronicles: Civil War Letters of the Bryant-Stephens Families of North Florida*, was published by the University Press of Florida in 1998.

My ancestor's letters, written in the early 1800s and never published, are part of a library's collections. Do I need the library's permission to publish them?

These letters would be in the public domain, and the copyright would have expired (taking into account the life plus seventy rule and that the ancestor likely died before 1935). But because the repository owns the letters and because they're one-of-a-kind, you may need their permission to publish them, and you may have to pay a fee.

If the copyright has not expired and the heirs (or the letter writer) did not assign copyright to the repository, then you would also need permission of the author or the author's heirs to publish them.

Who owns the copyright to a letter or an e-mail? The writer or the recipient?

The writer owns the copyright. If you forward an e-mail without the writer's permission, you are violating the e-mail writer's copyright. Since we know it's a fact of e-mail life that e-mails do get forwarded, it would be wise to never put something in an e-mail that you wouldn't want the rest of the world to know. E-mail is not private or protected. With a click of the mouse, it can be forwarded to hundreds of people. If the e-mail goes to someone's work, it can get archived in the company's files; if it's posted on a mailing list or newsgroup, it goes in an archive, and this is often publicly accessible. Think before you click.

Can an e-mail communication transfer my copyright to someone, even if I didn't intend it to?

While this is a question the courts will have to decide, to play it safe, if you are discussing rights and copyright with a publisher or editor via e-mail, include a statement saying that no rights will be transferred via this e-mail, and you don't have a legally binding agreement unless and until there is a signed agreement. According to the current Copyright Law, any transfer of rights needs to be done in writing and signed by the copyright owner.

Can I copyright my book, article, or lecture title?

Titles by themselves aren't copyrightable, but there are instances where someone else using your title might be guilty of "unfair competition." For example, say I've been giving a lecture at national conferences and around the country under a certain title for years, so that the genealogical public associates this title with me. If another genealogist comes along and uses that title (or a close variation of it) for her lecture, article, or book so that it causes confusion in people's minds, then it is not only unethical, but it can be considered unfair competition legally. According to Tad Crawford in *The Writer's Legal Guide*, 2d edition, pages 85–86, unfair competition can protect "titles which, although not usually copyrightable, may become so well recognized that reuse of the title … would create confusion of the new work with the original work." By using one of my lecture or book titles, another genealogist could be viewed as deliberately trying to confuse the public and benefiting unfairly from my reputation. There are several cases where judges have upheld the exclusive use of titles, even though the title is not protected by copyright.

If I enter my family history in a writing contest, am I giving up my copyright?

You would definitively want to review the contest rules and guidelines carefully. Look for any sections that mention owner-ship rights, publishing, or reproducing of your work. If entering or winning the contest requires you to transfer your copyright or rights you may not want to grant, rethink entering that contest. Some contests promise the winner(s)'s entry will be published in a journal. Before you enter the contest, ask to review the journal's boilerplate contract.

Is a collection of record transcripts, abstracts, a bibliography, or an index protected by copyright?

Only if there is a creative arrangement. Just an alphabetical, chronological, or numerical arrangement of preexisting material is not sufficient to make it copyrightable. While a bibliography would not be copyrightable, the annotation of an annotated bibli-ography would. Adding annotation to transcripts of records from other sources, such as biographical information, historical context, translations from a foreign language, or explanatory notes would make that part copyrightable. A name and place index wouldn't be protected, but add creativity, such as a subject index or identi-fying information to the names, and it can be protected. Keep in mind that the original materials—the bibliography, the tran-scripts, the index themselves—are not protected, only your origi-nal creative expression.

Who owns the copyright in an oral history interview?

Assuming the interview was taped, then the one who asks the questions owns the copyright to the questions, and the respondent owns the copyright to the answers. To use material from an oral history interview, you should seek written permission from the person you interviewed.

Someone told me that by mailing my manuscript to myself and keeping the unopened envelope with the postmarked date on it, that this is as good as registering my copyright.

This is known as the "poor man's copyright," but it's no legal substitute for copyright registration. The courts recognize only works registered with the Copyright Office.

Is it ever possible to reclaim a copyright assigned to a publisher or other party?

Sections 203 and 304(c) of the Copyright Act of 1976 allow for the ownership of a copyright to be reclaimed. If the work was created before 1 January 1978, copyright can be terminated fifty-six years after the date the copyright was secured; if it was created after 1 January 1978, it can be terminated only during a five-year window of opportunity between thirty-five and forty years after the transfer was made. Your heirs may also reclaim your copyright after you're deceased. Seek the help and advice of an intellectual property attorney if you wish to reclaim your copyright, as there are specific procedures to carry out this process correctly, especially if more than one author is involved and copyright is held jointly.

Is my work published and copyrighted in the United States automatically protected in other countries, too?

In 1886, a worldwide copyright convention was held in Berne, Switzerland, and was called the Berne Convention for the Protection of Literary and Artistic Works. Every country that signed the Berne Convention must give copyright protection to citizens or permanent residents of other Berne countries for at least the life of the author plus fifty years. The countries belonging to the Berne Convention include the United States, most of Western Europe, Canada, Japan, Mexico, and Australia. But, the United States did not join the Berne Convention until 1 March 1989. So, as Fishman writes in *The Copyright Handbook* (13/3): "The Berne Convention does not apply to a work first published in the U.S. before that date unless the work was also published in a Berne country at the same time (that is, within 30 days of each other). This is called simultaneous publication. Before 1989, American publishers commonly had their books published simultaneously in the U.S. and Canada and/or Great Britain (both Berne countries) so that they could receive the protection of the Berne Convention. This fact was usually indicated on the same page as the work's copyright."

Chapter 2
Fair Use, the Public Domain, and Seeking Permissions

At one time or another, we've all had a need to use another writer's words. You may be a book reviewer wanting to quote passages in your review. You may be writing a family history and want to quote from published or unpublished sources, such as an ancestor's letters and diary. You may be writing an article for a genealogical publication and want to quote an expert who's written a book on the subject. You may be teaching a genealogy class and want to photocopy an article relevant to the topic you're teaching to distribute to the class. Or, you may be doing research at a library and want to photocopy several pages from a book you've found on your family.

Are all of these situations OK to do without getting the author's permission? In some cases, yes; but in others, it may be copyright infringement. How can you determine when you need permission and when you don't?

DO YOU NEED PERMISSION?
Attorney Stephen Fishman, author of *The Copyright Handbook* (11/2), offers the following three questions to determine whether you need permission. If you answer yes to all three, then you need permission.

1. *Are you taking an author's expression?*

   You don't need permission to explain ideas or use facts, which can't be protected by copyright, but you do need permission if you're using an author's expression—"that is, the particular sequence of words." (Photocopying is always considered using another author's expression.)

2. *Is the author's expression protected by copyright?*

   Remember, copyright doesn't last forever. Any work published before 1923 is now in the public domain, as are many unpublished works, and anyone can use them without permission. Current copyright law protects an author's work (published or unpublished) for the life of the author plus seventy years.

3. *Does your intended use of the protected expression go beyond the bounds of fair use?*

   Now that *is* the question, isn't it? What is fair use?

WHAT IS FAIR USE?

According to Lloyd J. Jassin and Steven C. Schechter in *The Copyright Permission and Libel Handbook,* page 26, "Fair use is a privilege. It permits authors, scholars, researchers, and educators to borrow small portions of a copyrighted work for socially productive purposes without asking permission or paying a fee."

The Copyright Law of the United States of America, Title 17, §107 says to consider these four factors when determining fair use:

1. The purpose and character of the use. Is it for commercial or non-commercial use? Such uses as in reviews and commentary, news articles, teaching, personal scholarship, and parody are allowable under fair use without permission, but be careful. This doesn't mean you can quote extensively or make mul-

tiple copies to give to a class (see page 24) — you can still be infringing on another's copyright.

2. The nature of the work. The amount you can quote from a poem or song, for example, would be less than from a novel-length work. Also consider the type of work. It's generally easier to claim fair use from a newspaper than from a work of fiction.

3. The amount and substantiality of the portion used. If you've quoted the part that tells whodunit in a mystery, for example, even if it's only one sentence, it's a substantial part of the work.

4. The effect of the use on the potential market, that is, its economic value. Would the portion you quoted have an adverse impact on the market for the original work? In other words, are you quoting so much that there's no need for someone to buy the original? On the other hand, if the quoted material is properly cited and your use increases the likelihood that the reader will seek out the original, then it can help establish fair use.

However — you knew there'd be a "however," didn't you? — that same section of the law says that "the fair use of a copyrighted work ... for purposes such as criticism, comment, news reporting, teaching (including multiple copies for classroom use), scholarship, or research is not an infringement of copyright." What this means is you can quote from a work in a book review, you can photocopy an article for your personal research, and you can make copies of an article to distribute to your class without seeking the author's permission. All of these instances would fall under fair use.

Wait a minute. You *can* photocopy an article for classroom use and not have to ask permission? The reason this is sometimes

OK is because it's considered for nonprofit educational purposes. But—you knew there'd be a "but," didn't you?—you can't copy more than one for each student, each copy must include the copyright notice and the source it came from, it must be a short article of no more than 2,500 words, and the "idea to make the copies and their actual classroom use must be so close together in time that it would be unreasonable to expect a timely reply to a request for permission from the publisher or copyright holder" (Fishman, *The Copyright Handbook*, 11/11). So if you plan to use that same article next term, you'd better ask permission.

Be careful when putting together groupings of articles. If the instructor or a college bookstore binds and sells them to students, this might violate the fair use rules as they relate to classroom use.

Teachers may want to read an informative article, "Agreement on Guidelines for Classroom Copying in Not-For-Profit Educational Institutions With Respect to Books and Periodicals" at <www.cni.org/docs/infopols/NACS.html>. Likewise, librarians should become familiar with "CONTU Guidelines on Photocopying Under Interlibrary Loan Arrangements" from the National Commission on New Technological Uses of Copyright Works at <www.cni.org/docs/infopols/CONTU.html>.

HOW MUCH CAN YOU QUOTE?

Let's say you're writing an article or a book: How much can you quote from an author's work and still have it be within the boundaries of fair use? One hundred words? Two hundred words? More? Less? Ten percent of the work? Five percent of the work? Unfortunately, there's no magic number, despite popular opinion to the contrary. You have to consider the four factors stated in the Copyright Law. But two good rules to follow are

1. Would you have a problem with someone quoting that much of your work without asking your permission?
2. Quote only as much as is necessary to make your point.

If all this talk of fair use still sounds rather wishy-washy, I'm afraid it is. The real test of fair use is what a judge or jury would decide, but you don't want to let it get that far. It's always better to play it safe. Here's the simplified version of fair use: When in doubt, ask permission.

WHAT IS THE PUBLIC DOMAIN?
I already mentioned that any creative work is protected by copyright law for a given number of years, regardless of whether the author or creator is still living. But this protection does not last forever, and when the copyright expires, the work becomes part of the public domain. When that happens, these works may be used without permission and often without a fee. Some works are never eligible for copyright, so they are always in the public domain, such as works produced by the U.S. government.

Determining when material has passed into the public domain is *your* responsibility before you use it, and it's not always an easy task. But remember:

*   All works *published* before 1923 are now in the public domain and cannot be retroactively protected. Works published in 1923 are protected until January 1, 2019.
*   Many works published between 1923 and 1963 are in the public domain because such works either failed to affix the proper copyright notice or failed to renew the copyright registration in the 28th year; however, this should be thoroughly researched.

- U.S. government works created entirely by federal employees as part of their duties. (State and local government works aren't always public domain works, and the U.S. government may hold works wherein copyright was transferred to the government. In such cases, the work is not in the public domain.)
- Certain works commissioned by the U.S. government as works for hire, such as WPA (Work Projects Administration) works.

You are free to use any public domain works in your lectures, writing, teaching, and publishing without permission.

Unfortunately, there is no list or database of works in the public domain. You'll need to research whether a work is in the public domain by understanding the basic rules of copyright and checking the Copyright Office files (see pages 27–29).

You'll also need to ensure that any published version of a public domain work you want to use is the original and not an adaptation or revised edition. The adaptation or revision might still be protected by copyright. For example, Shakespeare's *Romeo and Juliet* is in the public domain, but there have been several movie and dramatic remakes of the original. The remakes would be protected. So if you want to reproduce, say, a map from the 1800s that you found in a recently published book, you need to make sure that map was not altered, making the published version protected. An adaptation or derivative work might be protected under a separate copyright, but the underlying original public domain work is still free to use.

Here are some questions to ask yourself to determine whether a work is in the public domain:

- When was the work created?

- Who created the work (an individual, two or more individuals, an employee of a business or corporation, for example)?
- Is the author still alive? If not, when did he or she die? (The Copyright Office keeps a record of deaths for authors of copyrighted works. See page 28.)
- When was the work registered or published?

After you answer these questions, refer to the chart in chapter one to see whether the copyright might still be in effect. Perhaps the best, most up-to-date, and easy-to-follow source is *The Public Domain: How to Find & Use Copyright-Free Writings, Music, Art & More*, by Stephen Fishman.

SEARCHING THE COPYRIGHT OFFICE FILES

First, establish whether the item is free from copyright by verifying the creation date, the publication status, and the ownership as mentioned above. If you've done that and still aren't sure about a work's status, you can check the records of the U.S. Copyright Office online to see whether a copyright has been registered and renewed since 1978. Go to <www.copyright.gov> then click on the link to "Search Copyright Records: Registrations and Documents." From there, choose one of the three options:

1. Books, music, films, sound recordings, maps, software, photos, art, and multimedia
2. Serials (periodicals, magazines, journals, and newspapers)
3. Documents

You can search by
- Author
- Title

- Claimant
- Registration number
- Map index terms and sound recording imprints
- All categories combined

For works prior to 1978, see the Online Books Page <www.digital.library.upenn.edu/books/cce/>. This database is not complete, so also look for volumes of the *Catalog of Copyright Entries*, published by the Copyright Office in print format from 1891 to 1978 and on microfiche from 1979 to 1982. You should be able to find copies of this set in law libraries and in some university and large public libraries to determine whether older works' copyrights were renewed and are still protected. A word of caution when using the *Catalog of Copyright Entries*: it does not contain assignment of copyrights, so if the copyright was transferred to another party, it won't give that information; and it doesn't list addresses of copyright claimants.

It's important to keep in mind that your search in these sources might not be conclusive. Unpublished works and those who chose not to register their work with the Copyright Office won't be included in these sources, so the work might still be protected. (See the chart in chapter one.) This is a good reason to make sure your work is registered. Refer to the Copyright Office's circular 22, "How to Investigate the Copyright Status of a Work," <www.copyright.gov/circs/circ22.html> for more help.

To determine whether an author who owns a copyright is dead, use the author search and type in the name. It will give you the birth and death year if that information was reported to the Copyright Office. Anyone with an interest in an author's copyright may notify the Copyright Office of an author's death.

Stephen Fishman in *The Public Domain* (1/11–12) offers this advice if you're still having trouble determining whether the work you want to use is in the public domain:

> If you do not intend to use the work to compete with someone's business, it might be relatively safe for you to treat it as being in the public domain. However, you should carefully consider the following two factors before deciding what to do:
>
> - the likelihood your use will be discovered, and
> - the economic value of the material.
>
> The smaller the chance of discovery, the more willing you should be to use materials whose public domain status is uncertain. Likewise, the lower the economic value of the materials, the safer it is for you to treat them as being in the public domain.

Fishman further states that "The chances of discovery are virtually nil if you use a work for your personal use or make it available only to a restricted group of people." If you're planning to publish your family history on the Web, the access is worldwide, of course, or if you're planning to donate it to a library, the access goes beyond a restricted group of people. When in doubt, seek permission.

HOW DO YOU GET PERMISSION?

When in doubt, it's always best to ask permission to reprint something in your book or on the Web. But whose permission do you need? The author's? The publisher's? Here's a breakdown:

- Books, commercially published: Write to the publisher for permission. Even though the author might still retain the copyright, in the book contract, the author typically assigns many rights to the publisher. Go to the publisher's Web site and look for a link for "permissions" or "contact us." Also, check the copyright page of the book for the publisher's contact information.
- Books, self-published: Write to the author. Self-published books might include contact information for the author on the copyright page or elsewhere in the book. Otherwise, you'll have to put your genealogical research skills to work to track down the author.
- Periodicals: Write to the editor; however, absent any publishing agreement to the contrary, freelance writers own the copyright in their articles, so you'll need to write directly to the writer. When a journal places the copyright notice on its publication, it is protecting the journal as a compilation, not the individual contributions.
- Photographs: Track down the photographer, especially for studio portraits taken since 1 January 1978 (see chapter three).
- Paintings: Contact the artist. Check to see if the artist has a Web site. Art galleries and museums may have contact information if the artist displayed his or her work publicly.
- Song lyrics: Contact the music publisher.
- Obituaries and news items: Write to the newspaper.
- Maps: Write to the map publisher.
- Internet: Look for a "contact us" link, or look for a link for the Webmaster/owner.

Remember, the author of the work may not be the current copyright owner. The copyright could have been transferred (assigned) to another person, to a publisher, or to a record repository, such as a library, archive, or historical society. Since copyright is intellectual property, it can be transferred in a will to anyone, including a record repository, or, absent a will, it can pass on to one or more heirs. Make sure you are contacting the rightful copyright owner. Here's where your skills as a researcher will pay off.

The Permission Letter

Permissions should be done in writing. Send two copies so the recipient can keep one and return the other copy to you. Here are the points your permission letter should cover:

- Title, edition, publisher, date of copyright, owner of copyright
- How you plan to use the work; what portion of the work you want to use, including page numbers where appropriate; the form your reproduction will take (printed book, Web page, etc.); the number of copies that you'll be distributing; whether your work is for commercial or noncommercial use (a family history is typically noncommercial); and the distribution and geography (among family members, to libraries, available in bookstores; in the U.S. or worldwide)
- What rights you are seeking (typically a nonexclusive license to use the portion in this one work)

Also ask whether there is a fee and what the fee is, as well as what credit line you need to use. Of course, it never hurts to include a self-addressed, stamped envelope with your request. Don't wait until the last minute to secure permissions. With some commercial publishers, it can take at least four to six weeks to process your request. And if you've inadvertently written to the wrong person and need to contact someone else, this can take more time than you expected.

APPLYING IT TO GENEALOGY

Is citing the source enough under fair use?

Sometimes it is, sometimes it's not. It's up to the courts to decide. Use the four factors of the Copyright Law as your guideline (pages 22–23). Regardless, *always* give proper attribution to your source. If you ever did have to go to court, it would be much more difficult for you to claim fair use if you didn't cite your source.

What about paraphrasing?

Paraphrasing is generally OK, but it depends on how much paraphrasing you do and how close your paraphrasing is to the original. You may recall a court case in 2002 involving historical writer Stephen Ambrose where he was accused of plagiarizing and paraphrasing too closely passages of Thomas Childers's book *The Wings of Morning.* In one part, Childers wrote: "Up, up, up, groping through the clouds for what seemed like an eternity…. No amount of practice could have prepared them for what they encountered. B-24's, glittering like mica, were popping up out of the clouds all over the sky." Ambrose wrote: "Up, up, up he went, until he got above the clouds. No amount of practice could have prepared the pilot and crew for what they encountered. B-24's, glittering like mica, were popping up out of the clouds over here, over there, everywhere." This is a little too close for comfort, don't you think?

Can someone put my research on the Internet without getting my permission?

Let's say you've spent years researching a branch of your family history. You've compiled the facts—names, dates, places—into one of the standard genealogical formats, such as the *Register* or *NGSQ* numbering systems. To it, you've added some analysis, biographical information, and some historical context. You're on the eve of publishing your book when you happen to be on a genealogy Web site and find many of those facts—names, dates, and places—in a database. Apparently a cousin, with whom you shared family group sheets over the years, took your data and submitted it to the database. Is this a violation of your copyright? I'm afraid not. Facts, such as those names, dates, and places, are not protected by copyright. What is protected is your creative selection and arrangement of the facts in your book.

If someone has put the creative portion of your work on the Web, then your copyright has been infringed. Often, sending a letter to the person telling her that you own the copyright to the material and please remove it is sufficient. But if not, you may need to hire an attorney to write the letter for you.

I've written to an author for permission to quote a paragraph from his book, even though I think it would fall under fair use. The author denied my request. Can I still use it?

Although this is a tricky one, if the quoted passage would indeed be considered by a court to be fair use, you might still be able to use the material even though the author denied permission. But while you might be able to do so legally, ethically, do you still want to? Not to mention, even though a court may decide in your favor, do you want to risk the costs involved in defending a fair use claim? If an author denies permission, respect his or her wishes, and refer the reader to the original or to a comparable source.

I've written for permission to reprint several pages from a book, but I've never gotten a response. What should I do?

First, make sure you've written to the appropriate party. For a commercially published book, write to the publisher. For a self-published book, write the author. Then, if it's been at least six to eight weeks since you sent your initial request, send a follow-up letter or e-mail. Your first request may have gotten lost in the mail or in cyberspace. If after another six to eight weeks you still don't receive a response, then you shouldn't use the material, unless you are relatively certain that it's material in the public domain. Paraphrase the material instead, or refer the reader to that source. If you are unable to determine its public domain status, document your efforts, then consider Fishman's advice from *The Public Domain*, quoted on page 29.

If a work is clearly in the public domain, but it's owned by a research repository, can I still use it without permission?

No. You need permission of the repository. Even though physical ownership of a public domain work doesn't entitle the repository to copyright ownership, it still has certain rights as the physical owner, especially if it is a one-of-a-kind item that no other repository owns. The repository is within its rights to deny access, publication, use, or to charge a royalty fee. Remember, physical ownership doesn't mean the repository owns the copyright, but it does mean it could charge a royalty fee. Whoever originally donated the public domain item may have also put stipulations on its use.

I realize I must use the original of a public domain work if I want to use it without permission, but what about a photocopy, micro- filmed copy, or digitized version of the original? Can I use one of these without permission?

Photocopies and microfilm copies typically aren't adapted or altered. They're an exact duplicate of the original. So you could use these without permission. A digitized version, however, may have been enhanced and altered, so you need to get permission from the person or company who did the enhancement to use that version. Or, go to the original yourself and make a photocopy or scan to use, assuming the repository holding the original has no restrictions on making copies.

Is everything I find on the Internet in the public domain since it's available to the whole world?

No! On the contrary, you should assume everything you find on the Internet *is* protected by copyright, whether or not you see the copyright notice. As mentioned, facts, such as names, dates, and places, cannot be protected, but the creative expression of those facts can be protected. Even a Web site's design is protected.

What about a family history I found on the Web that was pub- lished in 1886? That's in the public domain and free to use, cor- rect?

Not necessarily. If the person who digitized and uploaded the family history made any kind of enhancements to the original, the enhanced version of the family history would be protected by copyright. You'd have to find a copy of the original to compare.

The same would be true of pre-1923 newspapers, which more and more are being digitized and placed on the Web. You don't know what, if any, enhancements the Web publisher made. Find the newspaper on microfilm, photocopy the relevant pages, and use that copy.

I've written a family history and would like to encourage other researchers to use the material. Do I have to have it copyrighted?

No. You can donate your book to the public domain. To do so, on the copyright page, you would state that you are donating the book to the public domain, and no permission is needed to use material from it.

I found a lot of information on my great-great-great-grandfather on Ancestry.com. Can I print a copy of the Web page for my files, or to send to other genealogists in my family? He's my ancestor, so I own that information, right?

Just because it's made available worldwide to the public doesn't mean it's in the public domain. But you can download or print information from Ancestry.com, other databases, or GED-COM files for your personal use, just as you'd be free to photocopy pages from a book for your genealogy files. No one owns the information (facts) on an ancestor, since facts aren't protected by copyright. Although the facts aren't protected, the arrangement of those facts in the database is, making it a compilation.

Sending those facts from a database or GEDCOM to another researcher is probably OK, too, as "fair use," as long as you aren't distributing them to everyone and anyone or charging a fee. It's best, though, to give the other researcher the URL and have her print out the information herself.

Certainly, if you plan to publish something you've downloaded from a GEDCOM file, which is based on someone else's hard work, it would be considerate and ethical for you to ask permission. The same would be true of using any information, whether it's from a book, Web site, or other source.

Chapter 3
Illustrations, Images,
Photographs, and Maps

This chapter is adapted from Maureen A. Taylor and Sharon DeBartolo Carmack's "Free Art? Not So Fast," Writer's Digest *(September 2001): 31–33.*

One of the more challenging aspects of being a genealogist and/or writer is illustrating your work, whether in print or online. Most books are improved with relevant illustrations. If you're writing a family history, whether for your family or a client's, you'll no doubt want to include photographs, maps, or other art. Whether you seek art such as drawings, engravings, woodcuts, etc.; maps; photographs; documents; advertisements; or newspaper articles as illustrations, there are thousands available to you in the public domain that do not require anyone's permission to use.

As discussed in the two previous chapters, any creative work is protected by copyright law for a given number of years, regardless of whether the photographer, artist, or cartographer is living. Like books, articles, and unpublished manuscripts, protection for photographs, images, and maps doesn't last forever, and when the copyright expires, the illustrations become part of the public domain. When that happens, these works may also be used without anyone's permission and often without fee. Some images, maps, photographs, and illustrations are never eligible for copyright, so they are always in the public domain, such as works produced by the U.S. government.

Again, it's your responsibility to determine whether that map or photograph has passed into the public domain. Different rules apply depending on when the work was published and whether the material was published at all, such as most photographs. Any work published before 1923, including photographs and maps, is now in the public domain, and it cannot be retroactively protected. That said, you also need to ensure that any published version of a public domain work you want to use is the original and not an adaptation of the original. The derivative work might be protected under a separate copyright, but the underlying original public domain work is still free to use. (See chapter two.)

Using public domain photographs is also a complicated issue. There are public domain images you can use for free, but in some cases they are in private collections, and the owner can charge you a royalty fee for usage. So when is a photograph in the public domain? It depends on several factors, including whether the photograph is unique, whether it has been published, and the creation date. Keep in mind that a photograph does not require a copyright symbol to be protected under the law.

Copyright law says a photographer is considered the "author" or creator of photographic works and as such is the legal copyright holder. If you want to make copies of a photograph, alter it, or publish it, you need the photographer's permission to do so. Proceed carefully when using old images and other illustrations rather than assuming they are in the public domain. A photograph is considered "published" when it's made available to the general public, such as in a newspaper, book, or magazine; as a postcard or greeting card; or on a mug or T-shirt. A photo that is on public display is not considered published.

If you want to use a photograph taken or published after 1978, obtaining permission can be a simple procedure as long as you contact the current copyright holder. Send the photographer a letter requesting permission and outlining how the image will be used. In most cases, you will have to pay a royalty (usage fee) for the right to publish the image.

WHAT ABOUT HISTORICAL IMAGES?

While historical photographs published prior to 1923 are in the public domain, the situation is a little more complex. Before you use any historical images, determine whether they were ever published, i.e., made available for general distribution to the public, and when the photographer died. Under the 1978 law, unpublished works created prior to 1923, including photographs, are covered by special rules. If the images were published after 1978, then they are under copyright for an additional forty-five years or at least until 31 December 2047. Suppose you purchase an original image at an antique store. It was never published, the photographer is dead, and the image is unidentified. Can you use it? Attorney Stephen Fishman advises evaluating the risk in using unpublished images in terms of their economic value and the risk of being discovered. In many cases where the copyright status is uncertain, you may be able to safely use the picture. Again, when in doubt, contact an attorney for reassurance.

There are also ethical concerns with historical images found in museum collections. Even though the museum might not be able to claim copyright to these images and many are in the public domain, they can license you to use them and charge a fee. If it is a unique item, then you should pay the fee; however, if the photograph was published prior to 1923 and unaltered copies are available in other institutions, then they are in the public domain.

WHAT ABOUT USING FAMILY PHOTOGRAPHS?

If you want to use a family photograph, the copyright issues remain the same. Photographers hold the copyright for images; therefore, you can't use any professional studio photographs of relatives without getting the photographer's permission. In order for professional photographers to use your image in advertising or publications, they also need a release from you beforehand. Sample release forms and an explanation of rights appear in the *ASMP Professional Business Practices in Photography*. Not only are professional photographs an issue, but for any photo taken by a third party, the photographer owns the copyright.

Several professional organizations, including the Professional Photographers of America, have agreed to adhere to a set of copyright guidelines outlined by the Photo Marketing Association International. A complete set of the responsibilities of consumers and professional photographers is on the Kodak Web site <www.kodak.com/global/en/consumer/doingMore/copyright.sht ml> or in the *ASMP Professional Business Practices in Photography*.

Something Else to Consider

Look carefully at the photograph you want to use. If it contains any trademarks (such as on a sign in the background), copyrighted artwork (you ancestor is posing in front of a painting), or people, there's a good chance you're going to need additional permission. If you're photographing the house your ancestors used to live in and want to use it online or in print, you might need the present owner's permission.

USING PUBLISHED ILLUSTRATIONS, MAPS, AND PHOTOGRAPHS

Suppose you find a map, line drawing, engraving, woodcut, or photograph published in another book, newspaper, city directory, or elsewhere that you'd like to use. If the illustration is in a recently published work, then check the author's credits to see where the original came from. If it was originally published before 1923, then the illustration or map is in the public domain.

For example, I found an advertisement in an 1869 city directory I wanted to use as an illustration in one of my books. The city directory was on microfilm, and at the lead of the microfilm was a statement that no reproduction could be made without the permission of the "publisher." The publisher of the microfilm was identified as an antiquarian society. Although a city directory published in 1869 is clearly in the public domain, I nevertheless wrote for permission, thinking it merely a formality and that the society would supply an appropriate credit line. It granted permission but informed me that there would be a $75 reprint fee.

I questioned whether or not I had to pay a reprint fee because the work was clearly in the public domain. Ownership of a physical volume does not entitle one to charge a fee, unless that item is unquestionably one of a kind. This city directory was not a one-of-a-kind item. I found both original and microfilm copies of the same directory by other "publishers" in other repositories. Additionally, a microfilm copy is no different than a photocopy, and as such it would not be copyrightable because no creativity was involved or additional material added to make it a derivative work. I sought the opinion of a copyright attorney through the Authors Guild, who agreed that the work was in the public domain and that I didn't need permission to use the ad, nor should I have to pay a reprint fee.

HOW DO YOU LOCATE A PHOTOGRAPHER?

Along with typical sources such as telephone and city directories and the Web, try these organizations, although there are others:

42

American Society of Media Photographers
150 N. Second St.
Philadelphia, PA 19106
www.asmp.org

American Society of Picture Professionals
409 S. Washington St.
Alexandria, VA 22314
www.aspp.com

Professional Photographers of America
229 Peachtree St. NE, Suite 2200
Atlanta, GA 30303
www.ppa.com

WHERE ARE PUBLIC DOMAIN IMAGES AND MAPS?

There are thousands of images in the public domain for you to use to illustrate your written work. Check sources online and in libraries, archives, historical societies, and other repositories. Make sure the image you want to use is "copyright-free." Remember, a photograph or illustration does not have to have a copyright notice. While you'll find photographs and maps in U.S. government repositories, such as the Library of Congress or National Archives, that doesn't mean they are all in the public domain. You need to check with the repository on the specific image you want to use, and it's always best to make your request in writing.

If you're looking for copyright- and royalty-free clip art, Dover Publications (31 East Second Street, Mineola, NY 11501-3852, <http://store.doverpublications.com/>) produces many CDs and books with these types of images. Or, in your Internet search engine, type in "copyright free clip art" for other suppliers.

Maps created by the U.S. government are in the public domain. This includes maps created by the Bureau of Land Management, the U.S. Geological Survey (USGS), the U.S. Census Bureau, and other federal agencies, some of which might be deposited in the National Archives in Washington, DC. Maps created by state and local governments, however, might be protected by copyright, so always seek permission if you want to reproduce one of these maps.

Like other works, you need to determine when a map was created or published to know whether it's still copyright protected. Maps created in foreign countries are governed by the copyright laws of that country, which are different from ours.

WHAT ABOUT STOCK PHOTOS?

Explore these and other rights-protected and royalty-free image banks for finding photographs to illustrate your book or Web site:

Rights-Protected Image Banks
- Corbis: http://pro.corbis.com (it also has royalty-free images)
- *Time* and *Life* Pictures: www.thepicturecollection.com

Royalty-Free Image Banks
- Heritage Photographs: www.heritagephotographs.com
- Cyberphoto: www.cyberphoto.com
- Big Stock Photo: www.bigstockphoto.com

Also try typing "stock photographs" in your favorite search engine, such as Google. Keep in mind that even royalty-free images may come with a price for usage, but these are usually less expensive than rights-protected images.

APPLYING IT TO GENEALOGY

Can I use a photograph of a public figure in my family history?

Many of us have a famous person in our family history, but their being a public figure doesn't automatically put pictures of that person in the public domain. The photographer is still the copyright owner, or whomever the photographer transferred the copyright to (such as a newspaper or newswire service).

Another aspect to keep in mind is that public figures also have what is called the right of publicity, meaning they have the right to control how their identity is used because it has commercial value. Rights of publicity—which are governed by state law, not federal law—survive death by at least fifty years and can be enforced by the heirs. But the maximum in any state is one hundred years, so you can assume that a public figure or celebrity who died more than one hundred years ago isn't covered by the right of publicity.

I have a family photo taken about 1952. It's not a studio portrait, and no one in the family remembers who took the photo. Can I safely use it in my family history or post it on my Web site without permission?

Technically, no. The photographer still owns the copyright. But applying Fishman's advice regarding the economic value, chances are if the photographer comes forward, he likely won't sue you since the photo has a low economic value. At the worst, the person would ask you to remove the photo from your Web site or to not use the photo in reprints of your family history.

But, you have another issue to consider: the right to privacy, giving ordinary people the right to protect their identity and themselves from unwanted publicity. Those in the photograph who are still living may not want this image posted on the Web for the world to see or published in a book. You should also obtain written permission from those in the photo to use it. The right to privacy doesn't survive death, and it can't be enforced by heirs.

What about fair use? Does this ever apply to photographs?

You can use images for personal or educational use without monetary gain, subject to the same general fair use considerations as outlined in chapter two.

I located the photographer who took my grandmother's wedding picture, but he's deceased. How do I get permission to use the photo?

Check to see whether the studio is still in business. The photographer may have sold his studio, or a relative may have taken it over.

How can I tell whether an historical photo or document I find online is owned by a repository or is in the public domain?

Ask. Contact the library or archive. They'll be able to tell you whether they own the copyright to the image, and if not, who does. Keep in mind that most repositories charge a fee for use, even for some public domain images that may be rare or one-of-a-kind. As the owner of the physical public domain image, the repository has the right to charge a usage fee. If you want to share the photo or image with relatives, rather than publish it or post it to your Web site, give them the URL and suggest they take a look.

What about photos from Web sites, such as the Library of Congress site? Can I put one of those on my Web site?

Not without getting permission from the Library of Congress or the person who owns the photograph. The Library of Congress, as well as other government repositories like the National Archives, holds many collections loaned or donated to them by other archives, and not all of these collections were created by government employees. No matter where you find photographs on the Web, always ask for permission before sharing or posting to your own Web site, unless there is something on the site that says the images are copyright-free.

Chapter 4
Works For Hire

This chapter is adapted from Sharon DeBartolo Carmack and Roger D. Joslyn's "Who Owns the Client Report? What We Learned from Being Sued in Federal Court," Association of Professional Genealogists Quarterly *16 (June 2001): 137–140.*

Now these are words you don't ever want to see in conjunction with your name during your genealogical career. But Roger and I saw them, and I'd like to share with you what we learned about the ownership of a genealogist's report—be it a traditional report of your research, a compiled genealogy, or a family history book—from our experience of being sued in federal court over a dispute in the copyright. Through this experience, I hope to help you learn more about copyright and ownership of work you do for a client, as well as how to avoid problems.

Our story began like any other for a project of this sort. The client contacted Roger, wanting a family history traced with a fin-

ished product in the form of a narrative family history with genealogical summaries. Roger performed the genealogical research,
then subcontracted me to write the narrative. As creators of the
work, copyright was automatically vested in us, so Roger and I
signed an agreement between us that we would be joint copyright
holders in the work we created for the client. Unfortunately, we
learned too late that the client didn't understand anything about
copyright; our downfall was in not educating the client at the beginning and discussing the issue at the outset.

All was moving along smoothly through the research and
writing. The client loved what we were doing. The book went into
production. It ended up being a two-volume, "all my ancestors
back to the *Mayflower*," thousand-page tome, with a fully documented, illustrated, narrative family history in the first volume,
and fully documented genealogical summaries with analysis in
the second. (The client had also hired an illustrator.)

During the final phase of production, the project manager
queried us and the client about who owned the copyright. She,
like the client, did not fully understand the Copyright Law and
mistakenly assumed that because the client had commissioned the
project, that this was "a work made for hire," making the client
the copyright holder. But this was not the case. We said we owned
the copyright; the client claimed he did. Despite our explanations
of the issues to both the project manager and the client, as well as
citing the section in the Copyright Law supporting our claim, on
Christmas Eve 1999, we received a fax from the client's attorney,
asserting the client's right to the copyright. Not long after the 2000
New Year, we received notice that we were being sued in federal
court. The copyright was in dispute, and because copyright is a
federal law, it had to be heard in federal court. The client and his
attorney made an incorrect assumption about copyright ownership, and there was nothing to stop him from suing us.

WHAT THE COPYRIGHT LAW SAYS

Although the client and his attorney tried to claim that the commissioned work was a work made for hire so we couldn't be the copyright owners, under the Copyright Law it clearly wasn't a work for hire. According to the Copyright Law of the United States, Title 17, U.S.C. §101:

> A "work made for hire" is—
> > (1) a work prepared by an employee within the scope of his or her employment; or
> > (2) a work specially ordered or commissioned for use as a contribution to a collective work, as part of a motion picture or other audiovisual work as a sound recording, as a translation, as a supplementary work, as a compilation, as an instructional text, as a test, as answer material for a test, or as an atlas, *if the parties expressly agree in a written instrument signed by them that the work shall be considered a work made for hire* [emphasis added].

For an employer to claim an employee's work as its own under work for hire, the work must be "within the scope of employment." For example, a telephone receptionist who writes a book or a computer program (even if related to the general business of the employer, and perhaps even if done during "company time") would still be the owner of the copyright, and not the employer, since the writing of a book or computer program was not "within the scope of his or her employment."

In a work for hire situation, there is no need for any written assignment to transfer ownership to the employer. Essentially, the employer is the "author" and copyright owner automatically upon creation by the employee of the work in question.

There was no question that we weren't employees of the client. We were independent contractors, and for the client to claim us as employees, two key factors (although there are others) had to be present: He would have had to provide us with employee benefits, and he would have had to take out Social Security taxes from what he paid us, neither of which he did. A client can't treat a genealogist as an independent contractor for tax purposes, then claim that genealogist was an employee for copyright purposes.

Based on the second part of the Copyright Law, the client did specially order and commission the work, but in order for our work to meet the work-for-hire criteria with independent contractors, it would have to fall into one of nine specific categories mentioned on page 50 in item two. It wasn't a collective work, which as defined in the same section of the Copyright Law is "a periodical issue, anthology, or encyclopedia." It wasn't part of a motion picture or other audiovisual work. It wasn't a translation. It wasn't a supplementary work, such as an index. It wasn't a compilation as defined by the Copyright Law: "a work formed by the collection and assembling of preexisting materials or of data that are selected, coordinated, or arranged in such a way that the resulting work constitutes an original work of authorship. The term 'compilation' includes collective works." It also wasn't an instructional text, answer materials for a test, or an atlas.

Even if the work had fallen into one of these categories, for it to be a work for hire with independent contracts, it also had to meet the final criteria: "... if the parties expressly agree in a written instrument signed by them that the work shall be considered a work made for hire." This written agreement is crucial, and generally should be signed before work begins. Since we had no written agreement on this matter with the client and our work didn't fall into one of the nine categories, it clearly would not be considered a work for hire.

YOUR CLIENT REPORTS

Professional genealogists have long debated the issue of who owns the client report; however, the answer lies in §101 of the Copyright Law. Part of the confusion, besides the "specially ordered or commissioned" aspect, has no doubt been the definition of a "compilation." We often refer to our work as "compiled genealogies." But under the Copyright Law's definition of a compilation, a compiled genealogy doesn't fit. A compilation would include bibliographies, directories, and databases. An "author" would not make any changes to preexisting material, but would rearrange the preexisting material. Any added analysis of the material would therefore take a compiled genealogy out of the realm of a compilation as defined by the Copyright Law. Because the work we wrote for the client was a combination narrative/compiled genealogy with much analysis, it did not meet the definition of a compilation. Likewise, a client report would not be classified as a compilation for work-for-hire purposes, since presumably it is more than a recitation of facts; most genealogists' reports contain analysis. Therefore, the work a professional genealogist does for a client—unless it is a database—doesn't fit into any of the nine categories in part two of §101 of the Copyright Law.

WHAT IS THE CLIENT PAYING FOR?

Copyright is automatically vested in the author or authors of a work when they put their creation on paper or in other fixed form, such as an audio- or videotape or publishing it on the Web. So the minute a client report that you have written comes out of your printer, you have created something that is protected by copyright, and you are the copyright holder.

The client is paying for a service that involves your time and expertise. In exchange for the fee and for specially commissioning the project, the client has a *nonexclusive* license to use it. What this means is the client may use the work to publish an article or book, giving you credit as the copyright holder and author. The client may not make changes or additions to your work, however, without your permission. As the author and copyright holder, you retain the "right of integrity," meaning no one can make changes to your work without your consent. Nor can the client restrict you from using the work. You as the copyright holder and creator of that report may use it however you choose—in articles, lectures, books, for certification or accreditation purposes, and so forth—although you would want to take into consideration the rights of privacy of living generations. It would be courteous for you to have the client's consent, but it would not be copyright infringement for you to publish or otherwise use your reports without the client's approval. This is your right as the author of the report and as the copyright owner.

JOINT AUTHORSHIP

If your client works with you on a writing project and writes a portion of the work, then it could be considered joint authorship, depending on other circumstantial factors, including the parties' intent at the outset. The client would own the copyright to any expression he or she added to the work, so you might want to consider rewording those sections into your own words to avoid any joint authorship claims. Remember, if the work is deemed a joint authorship, then each joint author can exploit the work, and any monies received by one author are accountable to the other.

This means you would have to split profits 50/50, even if the client contributed only a small amount of the whole work.

WHY IS IT IMPORTANT
TO RETAIN THE COPYRIGHT?

We felt strongly that we needed to retain copyright to protect the professional integrity of our work. If we transferred the copyright to the client, then he would become the owner of what we had written, and we would have no rights to the work whatsoever. Think of it in terms of selling your house. Once you sell your house, the next owner can do whatever he or she wants to it. They can tear it down, they can add on to it, they can remove the porch, they can paint it purple with pink polka dots. If we had transferred our copyright, then the client could have removed our names and put his name on it as the author; or worse, he could have altered the text, making additions and changes that were wrong or inappropriate, then left our names on it. If our names are used, we need to know that the content is ours. Our reputations are linked to it.

Under copyright law, you can demand that your name be removed in the event of any misuse of your work, so as to avoid harm to your reputation.

THE LAWSUIT

The lawsuit set us back close to $20,000 in one year, even though we had one attorney, a litigator, working for us pro bono, another litigator giving us a discounted rate, and a third, an intellectual property attorney, working at her full rate only as needed. The cost of the mental anguish caused by a lawsuit is, of course, inestimable.

After a year of our lawyers' and the client's battling back and forth, of going through a pre-trial and two mediation sessions held in New York City, we could no longer afford to continue the fight and defend our position. So, we agreed to a settlement.

We agreed to transfer our copyright to the client in exchange for an *exclusive* license to use the work in the field of genealogy, meaning that we (and only we, not even the client) have this right. If the client decided to use the work in the field of genealogy (publishing an article based on our work in a genealogical journal, for example), we could sue him for infringement on our exclusive license. Because the client was concerned about the portions on living generations being made public, we agreed that we wouldn't publish those parts, nor would we publish the work in its entirety, but we would be able to show copies of the completed work to our clients; to use excerpts of the work not pertaining to living generations in genealogical and writing workshops, seminars, lectures, and classroom teaching; and to use excerpts of the work not pertaining to living generations in articles and books, both print and electronic, to illustrate writing and research techniques and as an example of our work.

EDUCATING CLIENTS

Our client mistakenly believed that if we owned the copyright, then we "owned" his family's history! A biographer who writes the life story of Martha Stewart doesn't own Martha Stewart's life. The biographer owns the creative expression of her life. We owned the creative expression of the client's family history.

We learned that before beginning work on any project, no matter how big or small, we need to discuss the copyright with the client and explain what this means. We believe that it's important for the professional genealogist to retain copyright in order to protect the professional integrity of the work we create. We make it clear that we own the copyright in anything we compose or create for the client. We explain why this is important to us—that we need to know what our names are on and whether our writing is altered. We let the client know that what he or she is paying for is our knowledge and expertise, and that the client will have a non-exclusive license to use our reports, giving us attribution. Then we put the understanding in writing for both us and the client to sign.

If a client insists upon owning the copyright, there is an alternative. First, raise your fee. The client needs to know that there will be an additional charge for the transfer of copyright. Your copyright is intellectual property, and as such, has a monetary value. Second, in the written agreement transferring your copyright, make sure there is a simultaneous license granting you the right to use excerpts in your career pursuits, excluding information on living generations (lecturing, teaching, writing, showing to potential clients, and so forth). Also include a clause that if *any* changes are made to your work, you must approve of those changes. If you do not agree with any alterations, then you reserve the right to remove your name from the work. This written agreement then needs to be signed by both parties.

You own the client report—whether it is a traditional report, a genealogy compilation, or a family history book—unless you willingly in a written document transfer your copyright to someone else, which you are certainly free to do at any time, even after the work has been completed. Your client report is not a work for hire, unless it falls within one of those nine narrow categories *and* you have a written document signed by all parties before work begins, stipulating that it will be a "work made for hire."

For more information on works for hire, see the following sources: "Working with Freelancers: What Every Publisher Should Know About the 'Work for Hire' Doctrine," by Lloyd J. Jassin, <www.copylaw.com/new_articles/wfh.html>; *The Copyright Handbook*, by Stephen Fishman, and *The Copyright Permission and Libel Handbook*, by Lloyd J. Jassin and Steven C. Schechter.

APPLYING IT TO GENEALOGY

If I write something for a genealogical society as a volunteer, who owns the copyright?

Unless you have something in writing transferring your copyright to the society, you own the copyright.

I'm paid to index our society's publication. Is that a work for hire, or do I own the copyright to the index?

While an index would fall under one of the nine categories (a supplement), for it to be a work for hire, you must have a written agreement signed by both parties before the work begins stipulating that this is a work for hire, unless you are an employee of the society and this work is within the scope of your employment. Otherwise, you own the copyright to the index, assuming there is some creativity to the index, and it's not just an alphabetical listing of names and places.

I've been asked to contribute a chapter to a book. Is this a work for hire?

Like the index question above, the chapter would fall within the nine categories (a collective work), but again, there must be a written agreement signed by both parties (you and the person or publisher asking you to make the contribution) beforehand that says this is a work for hire, which means you are relinquishing your copyright in the chapter. If no written agreement is in effect, you own the copyright to the chapter you wrote.

Is an article I write for a publication a work for hire?

Unless the periodical publisher or editor
- specially ordered the article,
- has a written agreement stipulating that the article will be a work for hire, *and*
- has an agreement signed by both parties before the article is written,

the article would not qualify as a work for hire. All three of these requirements must be met for the article to be a work for hire.

I signed a contract that stated my work was a work made for hire, but the work doesn't fall under one of the categories for a work made for hire. Is my contract valid?

There are cases where the court has held that the contract was a valid assignment, even though the type of work was not one of the work for hire categories. The theory is that the work for hire language in the contract showed the parties' true intent. So be cautious about signing anything that says "work for hire." Don't rely on the argument that the work in question is not one of those listed in the work for hire categories. According to the American Society of Journalists and Authors in its "Rights 101: What Writers Should Know About All-Rights and Work-Made-for-Hire Contracts," <www.asja.org/pubtips/wmfh01.php>, "Ultimately, a contract's validity is something that a court must determine, and courts often stretch to enforce the parties' underlying intent even where a contract contains some technical defect. Circumstances and contract language vary widely, so we urge writers facing this problem to speak with a good copyright attorney for legal advice."

Can I submit my client reports for certification or accreditation requirements without the client's permission?

Genealogical certifying and accrediting boards may require you to obtain the client's permission to use reports when applying. But based on Copyright Law, assuming you have not transferred your copyright to the client, you do not need the client's permission as you own the copyright.

Chapter 5
Collaboration Agreements

In the previous chapter, we looked at works made for hire. The importance of having a written agreement when it comes to any creative work you do, whether for a client or a society as a volunteer, can't be stressed enough. This agreement needs to clearly stipulate what's expected of each party.

A collaboration could be any of the following scenarios:

- You're commissioned to write a family history for a client.
- You and the client jointly work together on a project.
- You and a colleague join efforts to co-write a book, article, or work on some other project.
- You're asked to write something for a genealogical society, such as a brochure, booklet, or book.
- You and other family members join efforts to work on a family history book or project.

You can find sample collaboration agreements to adapt to your purposes in these books:

- *Literary Law Guide for Authors* by Tonya Marie Evans and Susan Borden Evans
- *Kirsch's Handbook of Publishing Law,* 2d edition, by Jonathan Kirsch

- *The Writer's Legal Guide,* 3d edition, by Tad Crawford and Kay Murray
- *The Writer's Legal Companion,* 3d edition, by Brad Bunnin and Peter Beren

The references above go into more detail on joint authorship collaboration agreements. As joint authors in a project, each party has the right to exploit the material. Typically, any monies received are split 50/50, even if one party contributed much less than 50 percent of the work. Make sure your contract specifies exactly what are each parties' rights and responsibilities. Below are the essential items to include in a collaboration agreement for a writing project with a client or for a society, assuming the client or the society is acting as the publisher. The agreement should open with the names and addresses of both parties.

Grant of rights and copyright

This is where you will stipulate who will own the copyright. If the client or society will hold the copyright, then this clause needs to stipulate what your rights to the work will be. It will also grant to the publisher (presumably the client or society) the right to publish the book. (See chapters six, seven, and eight for more information on various types of rights.)

Scope of the work

For example, if it's a book, will the work be one volume or two? What will be contained in the volumes?

Responsibility and ownership of materials

Will you turn over to the client or society all notes and photocopies of documents? Or will they stay in your files? If you need to buy books specific to the writing project and the client or society is charged for them, who owns them? Who will be responsible for providing the illustrations? Who is responsible for incidental expenses, such as telephone and fax charges, postage, etc.? Are those expenses built into your fee or will you bill the client or society? Who will pay for any reprint fees of copyrighted materials?

Manuscript

When will the work be completed? How often will you report to the client or society and provide draft chapters? Who has final say over the content? How many revisions are you willing to do? Can the client or society make changes to the text without your knowledge and consent?

Warranty/indemnity clause

This is a statement that both parties are free to enter into such an agreement, that the rights have not previously been assigned, that the work won't violate any copyright, and that both parties hold the other harmless in any claims.

Confidentiality

You agree that you won't make public any information about any living persons without consent.

Production phase

This section could be an addendum or part of the contract, but it details the phases of production: copyediting, page layout and design, proofreading, indexing, printing, and book binding. It should also specify that the client or society will be responsible for these costs, but you may want to include that you will make recommendations for which professionals to hire, and you will provide the client or society with estimates.

Publication and distribution

The client or society is publishing the work, but who will distribute it and absorb those costs? Presumably the client or society. Make sure this is clearly spelled out.

Kill fee

If the client cancels the project at any time, you should be entitled to a "kill" fee, meaning you get a flat fee if the project ends prematurely. The reasoning behind this is you have set aside many months—maybe even a couple of years—of your time to work for this particular client. That is income you were promised for a certain length of time. If that ends, how long will it take you to replace that income with another project?

Payments to the author

If you're working with a client, you will either charge by the hour or set a flat fee for your writing services. How will you be paid and when? Will you require a larger sum upfront to begin? Typically, you will not receive any kind of royalty if the work is self-published, so keep this in mind when setting your fee. If you're working for a society, presumably you are undertaking the writing project as a volunteer. Even still, will you receive any royalties?

Free copies

You will want to receive several free copies of the work not only for your personal library and portfolio, but to donate to repositories or send out for review. If the number of free copies to you becomes an issue, stipulate that the other party is responsible for donation and review copies, based on the list you provide.

Copies purchased by the author
You may want to provide copies for sale to students, audience members, or others. Can you buy copies of the book you wrote, and at what discount?

Revision and updating
How often are you willing to revise and update the work? What fee should you be paid? What happens if you are not willing or able to revise and update the work?

Right of termination
Under what circumstances, if any, can you or the client terminate the contract (such as the client not paying a bill you submit)?

Effect of termination
What happens if the contract is terminated? Do any monies need to be paid or repaid? How are your rights affected by the termination? Generally, all rights granted should revert to the author.

Independent parties clause
This is where both parties acknowledge that they do not have a partnership or any employer-employee relationship.

Infringement
What if someone infringes on your work? Who may sue, and who'll pay for that expense? Who recovers damages?

When you establish yourself as a writer in genealogy, it's half art and half business. The art is the writing, but your relationship with the client or society is business. There is a lot more to consider than the mechanics of researching and writing when you take on a writing project for a client or society. Having a written contract will forestall problems and instill trust and confidence in both parties. You want to do your best work, because it will represent you and your talents.

APPLYING IT TO GENEALOGY

I'm the president of a genealogical society. We're busy enough as it is. Why should we fuss with a written collaboration agreement with our volunteers for our society brochures and cemetery project books?

What happens if the person who's compiling your cemetery project decides that she owns it and doesn't want the society to publish it after all; she'll publish it herself? Or what happens if the society publishes it, then the member decides to publish the same work, competing with the sales of the society publication? As mentioned in chapter four, the volunteer owns the copyright, so she would be free to do with it what she wanted—unless there were some kind of written agreement where she either transferred her copyright or agreed to a clause preventing her from publishing it herself. A contract is meant to protect both parties.

I'm a professional genealogist writing a book for a client, and he is forever changing his mind about things at the last minute. What parts of a collaboration agreement should I especially fine tune to help with this problem?

Two important clauses are the scope of the project and the manuscript clause. These should spell out precisely what the project will cover and how many revisions you are willing to make. The contract should also stipulate that if these clauses need revision after the project is under way, then both parties need to agree to them in writing.

I wrote a "beginning your research" booklet for my state genealogical society. The society has a new publications committee chair, and without my knowledge, she "revised" the booklet extensively and had it printed, keeping my name on it as the author. She introduced erroneous and outdated information, and added "research tips" I would never suggest to researchers. Some copies have already been sent out, and hundreds more were printed. What can I do?

Assuming there was no written agreement between you and the society, you still hold the copyright to the booklet. Contact the society president and explain the predicament this puts you in. Also explain that you have what's called the "right to paternity," which ensures that your name as the author is acknowledged on your work, but that you also have the "right of integrity," which means that no changes can be made to your work without your consent. These rights, known as moral rights, are protected by law. Under Copyright Law you can demand that your name be removed from the work, as it would harm your reputation. This means that the society will have to destroy the print run.

Chapter 6
Journal/Magazine Contracts

Most genealogical writers, editors, and publishers realize that when a writer creates a manuscript, the copyright belongs to the writer. As you learned in chapter one, copyright is intellectual property, which can be sold or relinquished in its entirety or in pieces, the same as a piece of land can be sold or rented in its entirety or in sections. When you as a writer send your manuscript to an editor, one of two things will most likely happen: (1) you will receive a written publishing agreement asking you to grant certain rights (or pieces of your copyright), or (2) you will merely receive an acceptance letter, with no rights stipulated. (I'm assuming you're not going to receive a rejection letter.)

In the first case, read the agreement carefully to see exactly which rights you are being asked to grant. Remember, a publishing agreement is a contract, and contracts are negotiable. If you don't want to relinquish, say, electronic rights (more on this shortly and in chapter eight), then negotiate that item out or seek a compromise.

In the second case, when there is no signed written agreement, it is implied that when you contribute to a journal, you are granting one-time print serial rights. That is, you are granting the journal the license to publish your article once in the magazine.

Contracts don't have to be formal agreements for them to be legal and binding. Just an exchange of e-mails or letters will do the trick if you're granting only limited, nonexclusive rights, such as one-time rights. So make sure you understand everything you're agreeing to. Copyright Law requires that any transfer of your copyright (that is, all rights or an exclusive right of publication) must be done in a signed document. (For more on specific rights, see pages 71–73.)

Be extremely cautious of any agreement that asks for "all rights," "electronic rights," or "rights in any future media." Know what you are granting. If you grant all rights, this is like selling your home and the property on which it stands. You no longer have any claim to that property. So get the contract as specific as you can, and do not agree to broadly defined categories, types of uses, or terms.

There are three main reasons you need to carefully consider which rights you intend to relinquish:

1. You don't want your name used without your approval.
2. You want to reserve the right to use the material for lecturing, teaching, or in other professional instances, such as writing a book.
3. You need to protect your material from misuse by others.

By granting all rights, you lose control over these three issues.

I would also caution you to grant electronic rights or rights in any future media for only a limited time, say, a year to five years, if at all. Again, the issue is you want to be able to protect your work and know how and when it is being used.

If you granted electronic rights to a magazine or journal with no stipulations or without specifying *which* electronic rights (see page 72), that journal could theoretically take all of the articles you've written for them, without your permission, put them on one CD-ROM, and sell them as *The Collected Works of [Your Name*

Here]. Or it could produce a special-edition CD of several articles—yours included—on a single subject, again without your permission, if you granted electronic rights. While you may or may not have received monetary compensation for your work when it was published in print form, now that a special CD is being sold at a profit, perhaps you should be receiving a royalty. The bottom line, however, is that *no* use of your work should be made without your knowledge and approval of medium, format, and content.

Unfortunately, many writers don't care what happens to their material. They are eager to have it published and eager to share their findings and knowledge with other researchers. Ten, or maybe even five, years ago, I might have agreed with you. But with the turn of the twenty-first century, genealogy has entered a new millennium, too.

Our field no longer comprises only hobbyists and professionals whose first love has been to search for ancestors. Our field has become big business. CEOs and investors see a way to make a profit. Money talks, as we all know, and the small-time genealogical magazine you wrote for yesterday may be run by a corporation tomorrow. Remember, "Knowledge is what you get from reading the small print in a contract; experience is what you get from not reading it" (author unknown).

Fortunately, most contracts or publishing agreements today have only one size print, but the words can still hold surprises for both the publisher and writer. Regardless of whether you are writing for a small society newsletter or a scholarly journal, a publishing agreement is beneficial to both you and the publication, so there are no misunderstandings of what is expected of each party.

A publishing agreement can be as simple as an e-mail or letter between you and the editor asking you to write an article and stipulating the conditions, with your e-mail or letter responding that you agree to write the article under the terms stated in the letter or e-mail. While better than nothing, this type of informal agreement—or no written agreement at all—can lead to serious problems later on. With all the questions about copyright and electronic rights that have arisen in the past few years, contributing an article to a newsletter or journal is no longer a simple matter. It's best to protect yourself from any misunderstanding. Unfortunately, most writers and even some editors don't consider a written agreement until after a problem arises—then it's too late.

A good agreement will spell out everything, leaving no doubt in anyone's mind what is expected from both parties. It should also be fair to both writer and society publisher. You can find a sample journalism agreement on the National Writers Union Web site <www.nwu.org>. From the home page, click on "Journalists" in the left menu. Then click on "Standard Journalism Contracts." You can find this same sample in the *National Writer's Union Freelance Writers' Guide*.

DETAILS OF A JOURNALISM AGREEMENT
For a newsletter, magazine, or journal article, here are the essential parts of a journalism publishing agreement:

Introductory paragraph
This names the publisher and author and states what is expected of the author: the topic or tentative title of the piece, word length, and deadline.

Rights assignment
In our field, genealogical journal publishers are typically using only three types of rights for publication: one-time or First North American Serial Rights (a.k.a. first North American hardcopy print publication rights), Web rights, and CD-ROM rights.

Again, be cautious of contracts that ask you to grant "all rights," "electronic rights" without specifying exactly which electronic rights, or "rights in any future media."

Make sure you understand the difference between exclusive and nonexclusive licenses. Exclusive means that you're granting the sole right to use your work to one person or publisher at a time. If any exclusive rights are granted to any third parties, even you as the copyright owner are prohibited from exercising these rights yourself. Thus, not only can you not grant these same rights to someone else, you can't exploit them either, even if you retained overall copyright ownership. Be careful when granting exclusive rights. Sometimes it can be akin to conveying copyright ownership in that it can preclude you from doing certain things with respect to your own work.

Nonexclusive means you are granting the right to use your work but that you are free to make the same grant of rights to another party, even simultaneously. Exclusive licenses must be in writing and signed by the copyright owner; nonexclusive licenses can be verbal and terminated at the discretion of the copyright owner. Both licenses usually carry specified purposes and a specified time limit, which could be as long as the term of copyright (i.e., life of the author plus seventy years).

In chapter one, you learned that copyright consists of a bundle of rights. Here are definitions of some of those rights:

- **First Serial Rights**—This means you are offering to a magazine the right to publish your article for the first time in a periodical. All other rights are still yours. Sometimes you'll see "North American serial rights," which limits the rights to a geographic region. If you're writing a book, there may be a clause in the contract granting the book publisher the right to excerpt material from your book and send it to a magazine. These are also known simply as first rights or first serial rights.

- **One-Time Rights**—This means you are licensing to a periodical the right to publish your article one time. This is typically a nonexclusive right, meaning you can resell the work to another publication at the same time, usually to another magazine with a different audience.

- **Second Serial (Reprint) Rights**—Here you give a magazine the opportunity to print your article after it's already been printed in another magazine. Like one-time rights, second serial rights are nonexclusive. You can license second serial rights to more than one publication.

- **All Rights**—All rights means exactly that. You are granting all rights in the material to another party, and forfeiting the right to ever use that material again. Think carefully before signing an all-rights contract. You may want to use the work again, say in a lecture or as part of a book. Ask editors or publishers whether they will take first rights instead. If not, you might want to consider withdrawing your material and submitting it elsewhere. Also be cautious of contracts that reassign rights to the writer after a given period, such as a year. Do you want your material tied up that long?

- **Electronic Rights**—These rights cover a broad range of electronic media: CDs, online magazines, Web sites, interactive programs, etc. Make sure your contract specifies which, if any, electronic rights are included. The presumption is that rights not specified in a contract are kept by the writer, but if you sign a contract with the broad language of just "electronic rights," you're granting rights that cover all electronic media.

Proofhandling

In this paragraph of the contract, the publisher is telling the author that the article will go through routine copyediting; however, the contract should stipulate that the author will be given the opportunity to read and correct the edited version of the article.

Warranty and indemnity

In this paragraph, the author warrants that the work is original and that the work contains no material that is defamatory or invades someone's privacy. It also warrants that both parties have the power and authority to enter into such an agreement, and that each party will hold the other harmless should a lawsuit arise. This clause may be one of the most confusing and difficult to understand parts of the contract, and it could have financial consequences to you. Read "How to Deal with Indemnification Clauses" as <www.asja.org/pubtips/indem01.php>.

Compensation

Here is stipulated what the author will receive in exchange for writing the article and granting rights to the article, and when the author will be paid. Pay upon acceptance of the article (meaning an editor has reviewed the submission and agrees that it satisfies the terms of the contract) is preferred, but many magazines pay upon publication. Scholarly genealogical journals and most genealogical societies do not pay for submissions, but rather offer a set number of complimentary copies (usually two to six) of the issue in which the article appears.

Kill fee

A kill fee is what the author will be paid if the editor decides not to publish the article. While this is often a percentage (such as 25 percent of the original fee), the National Writers Union believes writers should negotiate for the full amount as a kill fee. The reasoning is that the writer has done the work in good faith and should be entitled to the full fee.

Reuse fee

Some magazines and journals do a "best of" or special editions of their publications and may want to reuse your article in print or electronic form. Make sure there is a reuse fee in the contract, which is usually a percentage of the original fee.

Signatures and dates

The last paragraph is where both the author and editor sign and date the agreement.

Realize that when you are offered a publishing agreement, you are free to question and negotiate it. A periodical or book publisher's refusing to negotiate a contract is a bad sign. If that happens, you need to consider whether you really want to be writing for that periodical. This is not to say that you will get everything you ask for. Negotiating means you may have to give on some things and compromise on others. But always ask.

APPLYING IT TO GENEALOGY

I wrote an article for a genealogical publication, and there was no contract. Who owns the copyright to my article?

You do. Absent a written agreement to the contrary, when a writer submits an article to a publication, it's implied that the writer is granting a nonexclusive license for one-time print rights only. Because the license is nonexclusive, the author may grant a similar license to another journal. Any other use of the article, such as reprinting it or putting it on a CD-ROM, needs to have the author's permission.

The journal I wrote for displays the copyright symbol. Does that mean I no longer own the copyright?

No. When the copyright notice appears on a journal, it signifies copyrighting of the compilation, not individual articles. You'll need to review your contract to see what rights you have granted. If you have granted all rights, then you no longer own the copyright.

I wrote an article for a journal many years ago before electronic media were even heard of. There was no written contract, but the journal (and my article) is now available on CD-ROM. Can they do that without my permission?

Absolutely not. If a journal has put back issues in any electronic form without written permission of its authors, then the authors' copyrights have been infringed upon.

Isn't archiving the journal on CD the same as archiving it on microfilm?

Not according to the National Writers Union or the American Society of Journalists and Authors. The ASJA's online article makes this quite clear. In "Electronic Publishing: Fiction and Fact" <www.asja.org/pubtips/ewrongs.php>, it says, "Microfilm, which replaced bound volumes, *was* a new form of archiving, containing each issue in its entirety, page after page, just as it appears on paper. But an electronic database, online or CD-ROM, is an archive of articles, not of issues. The publisher's copyright covers the collective work … but not the individual constituent parts. (Just as a writer's copyright in an article is for the stringing together of words; the writer doesn't own the individual words.)" A good example to illustrate the difference is *The New York Times* historical article database available by subscription through ProQuest. You access specific articles, not the entire issue for that day. Using microfilm, you see a particular day's issue in its entirety.

Chapter 7
Book Contracts

F or those who are writing books of record transcripts, guide-books, or reference materials, you might have the opportunity to work with a commercial publisher. If so, you should be offered a contract.

Never, under any circumstances, sign a contract that you don't understand. Make sure you comprehend every clause and the impact it has on you and the sales of your book. There are several books available that explain, clause by clause, a book publishing contract (see the bibliography starting on page 108). Even if you plan to hire an attorney to review the contract, you'll save yourself money and headaches down the road if you do some research yourself. And, if you do hire an attorney, make sure that attorney is familiar with publishing contracts; ideally, you want an intellectual property or publishing law attorney to review it.

By joining the National Writers Union <www.nwu.org>, not only are you entitled to free contract advice, but you also can download the *Guide to Book Contracts* from its Web site or request that a hard copy be mailed to you. By joining the Authors Guild <www.authorsguild.org>, you are entitled to free contract advice from a legal intern.

Be aware of one of the realities of book publishing that first-time authors sometimes don't fully grasp: the book publisher is buying your book. True, you are the author, but the book belongs to them, even though you still own the copyright. They are paying you to write a book they want to market and sell, so they have the right to dictate how that book needs to be written and published to be marketable. If this is something you have concerns about, then self-publishing, where you have full control over your product, may be a better choice for you.

If you have the opportunity to write for more than one publisher, you'll be surprised at the variation in contracts. Some may be as short as three pages, while others can run fifteen pages. Regardless, all should contain the following basic elements.

DETAILS OF A BOOK PUBLISHING CONTRACT
Grant of rights and copyright

Most publishers recognize that the author owns and wants to retain the copyright to the book, and the contract should stipulate this. Be cautious of a contract where you have to transfer the copyright to the publisher. Assuming you're dealing with a publisher that leaves you as the copyright holder, you will need to license certain rights from that bundle of rights, such as the exclusive right to produce and publish the book for the term of copyright (or a given number of years) and to sell it directly or through others. The contract should also stipulate who will register the work with the copyright office—usually the publisher does in the author's name.

Subsidiary rights

This is where you see what that term "bundle of rights" really means. If the publisher doesn't plan to exploit any of the rights specified under this section of the contract, it's best to negotiate them out of the contract. Or, ask for a "turnaround clause," meaning that if the publisher doesn't exploit certain rights after a given length of time, those rights will revert back to you. Rights stricken or not specified in the contract are reserved by the author, who may exploit them elsewhere. Each right you grant will offer some percentage of the book's sales as compensation (often 50 percent for subsidiary rights). To learn what the going rates are for these rights, see the *National Writers Union Freelance Writers' Guide* or *The ASJA Guide to Freelance Writing*.

Some or all of these may be specified in your contract:

- Motion picture and television rights. Few of us are going to write a genealogical book that will be turned into a motion picture or television show. Since the publisher likely won't use these rights, ask that they be stricken from the contract.
- Foreign-language rights. This is the right to have your book translated and sold in a foreign language.
- Audio rights. Like motion picture and television rights, audio rights may be another aspect to have stricken from the contract. The reason a publisher would want these rights is to put your book on audiotape or audio CD. But take a walk down your bookstore aisle and see how many genealogy books are sold this way. None that I know of.
- Performance rights. The likelihood of your genealogy book being performed is also slim. Strike from the contract.
- Electronic rights. As mentioned in the previous chapter, electronic rights encompass a bundle of uses and can mean Internet, e-books, electronic newsmagazines, CD-ROMs, DVDs, interactive software, subscription Web sites, or electronic media not yet invented. Do your best to get this clause more specific so you know exactly what rights you are granting. Also try to have stricken language that says "in any and all future media," since no one can predict what type of media we'll have in the future and what im-

pact that may have on the sale of your book. (Also see chapter eight.)

- Serial rights. These are the rights to excerpt your book for magazines and newspapers. (See chapter six for types of serial rights.)
- Book club rights. You'll want to keep these rights in the contract, especially if the publisher actively shops your book to book clubs. The only disadvantage is that while book club sales usually boost your book's sales numbers considerably, the book club buys the books at such a deep discount that your royalty percentage is often small.
- Novelty rights. These rights give the publisher the opportunity to license to a third party characters or other art from your book into T-shirts, action figures, mugs, and so forth. You might want to retain these rights and exploit them yourself.

Advance

Some genealogical publishers pay an advance; others don't. If you are offered an advance, it usually means it's an advance against your royalties. This means that you won't receive a royalty check until you have earned back the advance. Depending on the demand for your book, sometimes the advance money is all you'll see. The book may not sell well enough for you to earn back your advance. On the other hand, if the demand for your book is high, you have competing offers, or the first book made big profits for the publisher, you might be able to negotiate an advance that isn't against royalties. But this is rare in genealogy book publishing.

Usually advance money is split into two payments: you receive half when you return the signed contract and half when you deliver an acceptable manuscript.

Royalties

Royalties are a percentage of the book sales that the author is paid. Royalties are calculated and sometimes paid on net receipts, meaning the publisher's list price minus the distributor's or bookseller's discount. For example, if the list price of the book is $20, but the book dealer or bookstore buys the book at a 50 percent discount, paying only $10 per book, your royalty is calculated on that $10. So if you're getting a 10 percent royalty, you would receive $1 per book. Remember, book clubs and book warehouses, who buy the book in bulk quantities, get them from the publisher at deep discounts, reducing your royalty further.

Royalty rates vary, but the standard for hardcover nonfiction trade books is 10 to 15 percent. Paperback royalties can range from 7.5 to 15 percent. Some publishers pay an escalating royalty rate. For example, 10 percent on the first 10,000 copies sold, 12.5 percent on the next 10,000, and 15 percent on copies sold after that.

Royalties aren't paid on copies given away, such as those for review, or on those damaged in the warehouse or damaged or lost in transit to a bookseller. Some publishers withhold from the author's royalties a "reserve against returns." Publishers pay a royalty to the author on all books shipped to bookstores, but bookstores have the option of returning to the publisher any unsold books. So that the publisher doesn't overpay you on royalties, they reserve a percentage of your royalties for this purpose. This reserve is usually repaid to the author after a certain time period. Read your contract carefully to see what it says about this practice.

Most publishers issue royalty statements every six months. The contract should stipulate when the royalty period ends. If a royalty period ends, say, on June 30, you may not get your statement and check until a month or two after that, depending on the size of the publishing house and how many authors it needs to issue checks to. Just like contracts, royalty statements vary in their reporting from one publisher to the next. If you don't understand the statement, call the accounting department and ask someone to explain it to you. Usually there is a clause in the contract allowing you to audit the publisher's books, at your expense, if you feel there are errors in your statement. Often, however, a call to the accounting office will clear up any problems.

Manuscript delivery

This section of the contract should stipulate such items as the subject of the work, its length (usually given as a word minimum and maximum), how you should submit your manuscript (hard copy and/or disk), your deadline, and what supplementary materials the author is to provide, such as illustrations. Some publishers allow the author to prepare the index; others don't, and this will be stipulated as well.

Also in this section, it will specify that it is the author's responsibility to obtain permissions and pay any fees to secure them. Sometimes, authors can negotiate a budget for permissions fees.

The section of the contract that covers manuscript acceptance should be clear as to what is acceptable and what isn't. It should allow for you to be able to revise it if it's not acceptable. If the manuscript is still unacceptable after revising, then the agreement is terminated and all rights should revert to you.

Failure to publish

Typically all production decisions, such as title, cover design, back panel copy, price, trim size, format (paperback or hardcover and the type of binding), and the production schedule are almost always at the publisher's discretion, although most genealogical publishers will consult with the author on some of these items.

Contracts usually state that the book will be published between twelve and twenty-four months after you deliver the manuscript. If the market time is limited for your book, you may want to negotiate a shorter time frame for publishing. Some contracts may have a clause that says the book can be canceled because of a change in the market. If so, the contract should also state what rights the author has if the publisher fails to publish the book. Negotiate for a termination of the contract and reversion of all rights to you so you can freely shop the manuscript around to other publishers. You may also want to negotiate a retention of the entire or at least a portion of the advance, on the theory that the work has effectively been taken out of the market for some period by the publisher, thus possibly diminishing the overall returns and/or value of the work.

Also consider negotiating in the contract the right to purchase (at a significant discount) any proofs, plates, illustrations, cover art, or other items the publisher developed, should the publisher decide not to publish in the advanced stages of production.

Author's copies and discounts

The contract will stipulate how many free copies of the book the author will receive and what sort of discount the author receives to purchase more copies. Usually the author receives a 40 to 50 percent discount.

Warranties and indemnification

Just like a journalism contract, you will be asked to warrant that the work is original to you, that you're not violating anyone's copyright, and that your book doesn't knowingly contain any libelous or defamatory material. Be cautious of the wording in this clause. See "How to Deal with Indemnification Clauses" at <www.asja.org/pubtips/indem01.php> for suggestions on how to negotiate this part of the contract.

Option clause

This clause is also known as the right of first refusal on your next work. This means that before you can take your next book to another publisher, you must submit a proposal to your current publisher. Do not agree to a clause that requires you to submit a completed manuscript, nor should you sign a contract with language that binds you to the terms of your present contract. You especially want an "out" if you weren't happy working with this publisher. Or what if your first book sells well, and there's a big demand for it? You don't necessarily want to be locked in to that publisher and the terms of that contract. So either negotiate this clause out, or at least put a tight limit on the time frame to exercise this option, including a deadline by which the publisher has to respond to your next book proposal. Finally, make sure you can get out of the option clause if you're presented with a better offer from another publisher, and the first publisher won't meet that better offer.

Competing works clause

This clause states that you won't produce a competing work to the one you are writing. It wouldn't be in your best interest to put out a similar book and be in competition with yourself. (Ironically, you won't find any publisher willing to agree not to produce a work that would compete with your book!)

Out of print clause

In this section, it should define what "out of print" means. Typically, the contract will say that a work is out of print if it is no longer available through normal retail channels in the United States. A word of caution: Electronic versions never go out of print, nor do books that are published as "print on demand."

The contract should stipulate what happens when your book goes out of print; presumably, all rights revert back to you, and you're free to take your book to another publisher.

Remaindering

When a book is declared out of print, it doesn't mean that there isn't any stock left. It means that the publisher is not going to print any more copies of the book, usually because there is an overstock, and based on past sales, the publisher anticipates that it will take too long to sell the remaining copies. So it remainders the book, putting the remaining stock up for bid to booksellers. Bookstores can bid on and buy the entire stock or a portion of the stock, usually at the publisher's cost to print the book. These are the "bargain" books you see at bookstores.

The publisher will still continue to sell any remaining stock at full price or at a discount, however, and will continue to pay the author the contracted royalty. Sometimes it can take a year or more for the overstock to be sold off, which means that even though the book is deemed out of print, the book might still be available, and the author still receives semi-annual royalty checks.

The author is normally notified when a book is being taken out of print and remaindered, and usually given the opportunity to purchase all or some of the copies at the publisher's cost— sometimes just a couple of dollars a copy.

Revised editions

This clause states how often the book might be revised and what you'll be paid to do the revision. Most publishers will not revise a book unless the material has become dated, the author

can provide at least 20 percent new material, and the book has a
good sales history.

Marketing obligations of the publisher

Many publishers won't agree to any firm commitments in the
contract, but some will. Even if you can't get it into the contract,
it's a good discussion to have with the publisher to get a sense of
what efforts they plan to make on your behalf, such as putting ads
in magazines, making the book available at conferences, sending
out flyers or brochures, featuring it as a new book in its catalog,
and so forth.

APPLYING IT TO GENEALOGY

*I've been offered a book contract. What's the best way to negoti-
ate it?*

As mentioned in chapter six, all contracts are negotiable, or
should be. Never sign the boilerplate contract. The best way to
negotiate is to put your thoughts or requests in writing. Either
have your notes ready and call the person who sent you the contract, or send that person an e-mail with your questions and requests. The publisher who offered you a contract *wants* to work
with you, otherwise they wouldn't have offered you a contract. So
don't be shy or intimidated. You may not get everything you ask
for, but always ask. Be prepared to give on some items and compromise on others. If there is a "deal breaker," meaning there is
something in the contract that is totally unacceptable to you, let
the publisher know. But keep in mind that some items are simply
non-negotiable in a book publishing contract, such as the war-
ranty clause. That said, however, you might be able to add wording, as suggested by the American Society of Journalists and

Authors <www.asja.org/pubtips/indem01.php>, that provides additional context to make you more comfortable with the language. It never hurts to ask.

How long can I take to review the contract and negotiate it?

Most publishers expect that you will take a few weeks to review a contract and seek advice from a third party, such as an attorney or author's representative. Contracts can take a couple months to negotiate, so make sure your manuscript delivery deadline takes this into account. You don't want to have your manuscript due almost immediately after you've signed the contract, unless you already have a completed manuscript.

What is the difference between engaging a lawyer vs. a union contract advisor?

The main difference is that the lawyer will be able to negotiate the contract for you if you don't feel comfortable doing that part yourself. National Writers Union contract advisors won't be able to negotiate your contract, but they will be able to tell you how to negotiate it yourself and what kind of language you should substitute for clauses that aren't in your best interests. Be aware that union contract advisors are not liable or responsible for the outcome of your contract.

Do I need an agent?

While some genealogists do have agents, one isn't necessary in our field if you're planning to work with one of the established genealogical publishers. A writer engages an agent to find a publisher and then negotiate the contract. In return, the agent receives a percentage of the author's advance and royalty, usually 15 percent, for the lifetime of the book. In our field, there is no reason to have this intermediary. It only cuts into your earnings. If you are looking for an agent to review and negotiate your contract, you're better off paying a one-time fee to an attorney than 15 percent of your earnings for the rest of the book's shelf life.

Chapter 8
Electronic Contracts

Electronic publishing is still a new frontier, but standard copyright laws apply to electronic rights as well. No doubt the laws will change and evolve over the years to accommodate this new technology. Think about it. When our founding fathers wrote the first copyright laws, the "new" technology of photography hadn't even been born yet. But the laws still applied and eventually were adapted to protect photographers' rights.

As you've read in previous chapters, electronic rights consist of a bundle of uses and can encompass the following media:

- E-books
- Databases
- DVDs
- CDs
- Software
- Multimedia and interactive software
- Subscription and non-subscription Web sites
- E-newsletters and magazines
- Reprint services
- Archival databases
- Print-on-demand publishing (see chapter nine)
- Technology and media not yet discovered

Make sure you understand whether the publisher will be producing the electronic media itself or licensing the electronic rights to a third party. Or you may be negotiating directly with a publisher that produces only electronic media. Three organizations offer advice, standard rates, and negotiation strategies on their Web sites for non-members to read: National Writers Union <www.nwu.org>, American Society of Journalists and Authors <www.asja.org>, and Authors Guild <www.authorsguild.org>. If you do a lot of writing or contributing to electronic media (such as databases and online magazines), it would be beneficial to you to explore these sites for the wealth of information they contain, as well as joining one or all of them for even more information.

Electronic uses are different from print in that they can be around forever; they never go out of print. Whether you're writing a book or an article, the electronic contract should contain all of the same components as print contracts, but the electronic contract should be explicit in its electronic usage clause. *Writing.com,* by Moira Anderson Allen, is an indispensable book if you plan to do any kind of writing for publication on the Web. Read especially chapter eight, "Protecting Your Electronic Rights." When reviewing a contract for electronic rights, consider the following:

- Make sure the electronic rights you are granting are specific and spelled out. If you are selling electronic rights, each use should be negotiated separately. Be cautious of an "all-electronic-rights" clause.
- Try to limit the duration of the license for electronic rights, say, to a year.
- Grant rights only to media now known to exist, not to any "future media."
- The contract should spell out conditions for any abridgement or anthologizing of your work or the addition of il-

lustrations, sound, or computerized effects—such as animation or hypertext links.

- All fee and non-fee uses should be stated and what royalty percentage you'll receive if your work is posted on a fee (or subscription) Web site.
- Realize that archival rights could tie up your work indefinitely unless they are nonexclusive, which means you can offer it to another electronic site. So make sure the rights are nonexclusive or there's a time limit on how long the work can be archived.
- Clarify whether the publisher will be producing the electronic media or licensing it to a third-party publisher.

Understand that there is a difference between *licensing fees* and *royalties*. A royalty is an amount paid to the author by the publisher. If the print publisher is also the electronic publisher, then the author should receive at least a traditional royalty on the electronic version. If you grant to the print publisher electronic rights with no stipulations, then your book can be put in any type of electronic form without your consent. Your contract should still specify a royalty for each electronic use.

A license is where the print publisher sells or licenses secondary rights, such as electronic rights, to another publisher, which could be done without your knowledge or consent if you granted electronic rights without stipulations to the print publisher.

POSTING YOUR WORK ON THE WEB

Whether you're working with a publisher or you're creating your own Web site to post articles and research findings, Lee Wilson in *The Copyright Guide*, pages 176–178, offers this sage advice:

Think about how likely it is that what you put into cyberspace will be stolen or further disseminated. Unless you are willing, in effect, to surrender your copyright rights in your work, think twice about putting it into an "instant-infringement" form…. There are not yet enough reported court decisions to say exactly what the law is in every situation…. Until the cyberspace frontier has been settled, be cautious about what you park in its commercial district….

Bringing an infringement lawsuit against an offender is costly, and if you're working with a publisher, that publisher is under no obligation to sue on your behalf, even though your contract may have an infringement clause. The publisher recognizes that lawsuits are expensive to pursue, and it may not consider your case to be profitable enough. Give it serious thought before posting your work on the Web.

APPLYING IT TO GENEALOGY

How can I copyright my Web site or online database?

Online at the Copyright Office site, look for the informational circular number 66, "Copyright Registration for Online Works" <www.copyright.gov/circs/circ66.html>. This will walk you through the steps of registering your Web site and other online work.

Can I register my domain name for copyright protection?

Copyright law doesn't protect domain names. Although beyond the scope of this book, registration and use of domain names can impact other issues such as trademark, publicity, privacy, defamation, and unfair competition issues, so if you have questions regarding use and registration of domain names, it's best to seek the advice of an attorney.

The Internet Corporation for Assigned Names and Numbers <www.icann.org/>, a nonprofit organization, has assumed the responsibility for domain name management.

Isn't making an electronic copy of something the same as making a photocopy or microfilming it?

It depends. If the electronic copy is merely a scan and no enhancements are done to it, then it would be the same as making a photocopy or microfilming it. But if the image is enhanced in any way, taken out of its context (such as an article separated from the journal in which it appeared and reproduced), or has hyperlinks or graphics added to it, then something new has been added, making it a derivative work. Keep in mind the other rights in the bundle, too. For example, by posting something on a Web site, you could be violating distribution and dissemination rights of the copyright holder.

If I publish an article I've written on my own Web site, have I forfeited first rights?

First rights typically refers to First North American Serial Rights in a print publication. But by self-publishing the article online, some publishers might consider this first publication. If you want to send the article to a print publication after making it available online, make sure the contract stipulates one-time rights. The danger is that the print publisher may offer you a reprint fee rather than the full fee for first rights. It's better to post on your site only articles that have already been published, assuming you still hold the rights to do so.

How would I know whether content from my Web site has been plagiarized? One can't police the Internet!

Try searching at Copyscape: Online Plagiarism Protection to find whether copies of your content is on the Internet <www.copyscape.com>. You can also use free banners from this site to put on your own site as a warning to others not to copy your site. But you should also routinely do a search in Google or another search engine on your name or article, book, and lecture titles, just to see what's out there. Moira Anderson Allen's *Writing.com* offers sample letters to send to infringers.

Are databases protected by copyright?

Yes and no. Databases are comprised of two parts: (1) the facts and data, and (2) the database software. The facts and data in a database cannot be protected. If the database's software is original and has even a minimal amount of creativity in its selection or arrangement of the data, then the database software is protected. If, on the other hand, the database software merely arranges the data into an alphabetical listing of people in a group of records (similar to an index), then it would not be protected.

Chapter 9
Self-Publication Contracts

While we all dream of being commercially published, sooner or later, almost all genealogists end up publishing their own books, whether these are family histories, record transcripts or abstracts, or reference guides. To do so, you might engage the services of a "vanity press," "subsidy press," or "print-on-demand" (POD) publisher, where you, the author, pay to a book printer all costs of producing the book.

Doing it yourself—that is, preparing the camera-ready print or electronic copy and contracting with a small-print-run publisher—has the benefit that you retain complete control over your project. You'll make all the decisions about how the book will look, what title it gets, how much to sell it for, whether it will be hardcover or paperback, and so on. Of course, to have all this control, you pay all the costs for the publication, marketing, and distribution of your book.

Even though you're in control, you'll still need to have a written contract with the book printer or POD publisher. These contracts usually aren't as detailed as ones with commercial publishers, but you'll want to make sure certain items are covered in your contract. (For more information on subsidy publishing contracts, see Tom and Marilyn Ross's *The Complete Guide to Self-Publishing*, 4th edition.)

Camera-ready or electronic files

While you'll still find some publishers who will accept camera-ready copy (that is, a high-quality print out of your manuscript from which they can make reproductions), most will prefer an electronic copy in a PDF format. If you can't supply your manuscript as a PDF file, for a fee, the publisher might be willing to convert it for you.

Number of copies

The greater the number, the lower the cost per copy. But do you want five hundred copies of a family history sitting in your garage if you can't sell them all? Some small-print-run publishers, however, have a minimum that you have to print. It may be as few as twenty-five or as many as one hundred. The contract needs to stipulate how many copies you want to have printed.

Paper quality and binding

Will the printer use archival-quality paper or regular bond paper? What kind of stock and weight? Will a different quality of paper be used for pages with photographs? Will the book be printed in hardcover or paperback?

Trim size

Books come in a variety of sizes. Make sure you're familiar with the size you choose for your book, and that it won't be unwieldy with the number of pages you have included.

Number of illustrations

The more illustrations the printer has to deal with, the higher the cost. The contract should stipulate how many illustrations you plan to submit and the cost for reproducing them.

Lead time and delivery date

A publisher who specializes in family histories has two busiest times: right before summer (for family reunions) and a couple months before Christmas. If your goal is to have a book for either of those two events, you need to have your camera-ready manuscript or disk to the printer several months in advance. The contract should specify when you need to deliver the pages and illustrations, and when the printer will be able to deliver the completed book to you.

Shipping

More than likely, you'll pay the shipping costs, but who will be responsible if the books get lost or damaged during shipping?

Payment terms

How much must you pay up front, and when is the balance due? Are payment plans an option? What major credit cards do they accept?

Proofs or "blue lines"

You should be given the opportunity to review final page proofs (sometimes still called "blue lines" or, in today's technological capabilities, digital proofs) of all parts of the book: cover, interior text, and back cover panel. Keep in mind that any changes at this point are costly, so if you have the urge to insert a missing comma, you may want to rethink whether it's worth the price to have that comma there.

Termination agreement

You should have the right to terminate the contract for any reason *before the printer begins work*. If work has begun, however, the contract needs to cover the circumstances under which the contract can be terminated, if any.

Late shipment or failure to deliver

What happens if the publisher doesn't deliver your books in time for the family reunion or for your speaking engagement? What recourse do you have? The contract should spell this out.

PRINT-ON-DEMAND PUBLISHING

Today, you have another option for publishing your work besides the small-print-run publisher. It's called print-on-demand publishing or POD. Print on demand means the publisher stores your book electronically and prints it only when someone orders one — or you can order as many copies at a time as you want to sell. Some POD publishers have a lengthy turnaround time (about four to six weeks) to publish a book because they subcontract the printing to another firm; others have their own printing equipment and can turn books out in less than forty-eight hours.

Advantages of POD

The advantages of publishing your family history through POD are many:

- You won't have to subsidize publishing more books than you need.
- You won't have to find a place to store a multitude of copies that you haven't been able to sell or distribute yet.
- You won't have to handle the sales or the shipping.
- It's less expensive than traditional small-print-run publishing.
- Some POD publishers pay authors a royalty.
- POD publishers usually offer step-by-step instructions on how to prepare your book for publication as part of their services.

- Some provide a list of freelance editors and typists.
- Authors typically get a discount on copies they purchase.
- Many POD publishers let you keep all rights to your book.
- Some offer marketing packages to help sell your book.

The main disadvantage of POD publishing is you may not be able to find one who will print on archival-quality paper or do the kind of long-lasting binding or covers you want.

Make sure you do your homework on the POD publisher you choose. Find out about rights, costs, when royalties will be paid, author's discounts, and what happens if the publisher goes out of business. Some POD publishers print their contracts online. Your written agreement with the POD publisher needs to cover all the items above, plus it needs to have an option to terminate your agreement should you decide to cease publication of your work — that is, you want to take it out of print. Again, see *The Complete Guide to Self-Publishing* and *Writing.com* for more advice on electronic publishing.

Your POD contract should also cover

- assigning an ISBN [International Standard Book Number, which helps booksellers find your book].
- providing you with proof copies.
- providing copies and forms so you can register your book with the Copyright Office.
- marketing and promotional options, such as adding your book to the publisher's online catalog, listing it in *Books in Print* and with online booksellers, and sending out review copies.

THE BOILERPLATE CONTRACT

Whether you're working with a traditional book printer or POD publisher, always ask to see its boilerplate contract when you write for a price quote. Like other contracts, it should be negotiable. If the publisher or printer doesn't have a contract, look for another one that does. And above all, don't sign anything you don't understand!

APPLYING IT TO GENEALOGY

I've never published a book before, and the printer I selected sent me a boilerplate contract. I don't know anything about paper weights and types or what size book makes sense for my family history. Where can I get advice on these details?

The printer should take the time to answer any questions you have, sending you sample papers and giving you guidance on producing your book. If not, perhaps you need to find another printer. Also refer to books like *The Complete Guide to Self-Publishing*, and talk with others who've published their own family history.

I'm eighty years old and self-publishing my first family history book. Is there anything I should include in the contract or the book to make it easy for my daughter to publish more copies after I'm gone?

In your will, designate your daughter as your "literary executrix," giving her the power to carry out your wishes for your book. You can also stipulate that she is your representative in your contract. Making her the literary executrix does not mean she automatically becomes the owner of the copyright, however, unless she is your only heir. So you might also want to consider transferring your copyright to her in your will. See a probate attorney for advice.

If I contract with a POD publisher, can I switch to a regular print publisher if I find there is more interest in my book than I expected?

Make sure there is something in your contract with the POD publisher that allows you to terminate your agreement at any time; however, if the POD publisher is paying you a royalty, you may not want to switch to a subsidy publisher, who may not pay royalties.

There are so many POD publishers and print publishers out there. How do I possibly choose?

Talk with other people in your genealogical society or friends who've self-published their family history. What press did they use? Were they happy working with that publisher? Also look for small-print run publishers who advertise in genealogical publications, such as *Family Tree Magazine, Ancestry, Heritage Quest,* and others. These companies are accustomed to working with genealogies that come heavy with source citations. Get bids from at least three companies. Most are happy to provide you with a no-obligation price quotation.

Glossary

advance. Money paid to the author to write a book, usually upon signing the contract, as an advance against future royalties.

all rights. A grant of all rights in a work to another party, and forfeiting the right to ever use that material again without that party's permission.

assignment of copyright. The transfer of all exclusive rights in a copyright to another party. (See transfer of copyright.)

author. The creator of a work. The term "author" is used for all creators, whether they be writers, photographers, artists, graphic designers, etc.

collaboration agreement. A contract between two or more parties to create a work.

collective work. "A work, such as a periodical issue, anthology, or encyclopedia, in which a number of contributions, constituting separate and independent works in themselves, are assembled into a collective whole." (Copyright Law of the United States of America §101)

compilation. "A work formed by the collection and assembling of preexisting materials or of data that are selected, coordinated, or arranged in such a way that the resulting work as a whole constitutes an original work of authorship. The term 'compilation' includes collective works." (Copyright Law of the United States of America §101)

copyright: A federal law dating to the writing of the U.S. Constitution. It gives the creator of the work the exclusive legal right to decide how the work will be used.

created. "A work is 'created' when it is fixed in a copy ... for the first time...." (Copyright Law of the United States of America §101)

database. A collection of preexisting material arranged in a searchable electronic format.

derivative work. "A work based upon one or more preexisting works, such as a translation, ... fictionalization, ... sound recording, abridgement, condensation, or any other form in which a work may be recast, transformed, or adapted...." (Copyright Law of the United States of America §101)

electronic rights. Rights that cover a broad range of electronic media: print-on-demand publishing, e-books, e-newsletters, Web sites, CD-ROMs, DVDs, interactive software, archival databases, etc.

exclusive license. A transfer or assignment of one or more rights, but not all rights, to another party. The party holding an exclusive license becomes the owner of those rights and can sue if there is an infringement on those rights.

fair use. The privilege to quote or use a portion of a copyright-protected work without the author's permission.

first serial rights. The right to publish an article for the first time in a periodical. Sometimes referred to in the United States as "First North American Serial Rights."

fixed form. "A work is 'fixed' in a tangible medium of expression when its embodiment in a copy or phonorecord, by or under the authority of the author, is sufficiently permanent or stable to permit it to be perceived, reproduced or otherwise communicated for a period of more than transitory duration...." (Copyright Law of the United States of America §101)

grant of rights. The clause in a publishing agreement that lists what rights the author is granting to a publisher, usually the right to publish the work.

independent contractor. A person who works independently from an employer.

joint work. "A work prepared by two or more authors with the intention that their contributions be merged into inseparable or interdependent parts of a unitary whole." (Copyright Law of the United States of America §101)

kill fee. The fee paid to an author should the publisher decide not to use the work under contract.

literary executor/executrix or representative. The person designated in the author's will to handle the author's intellectual property. This person would not own the copyright to the author's works, unless the author made a provision in the will transferring his or her copyright to the literary executor or representative.

nonexclusive license. A grant of a right or rights to another party on a nonexclusive basis. The copyright holder may still use or grant these same rights to another party.

one-time rights. A nonexclusive license granting a publisher the right to publish an article one time.

originality. For copyright purposes, this means that a work cannot have been copied from a preexisting work.

print on demand. A form of subsidy book publishing where copies are printed only when there is a request for them.

publication. "The distribution of copies or phonorecords of a work to the public by sale or other transfer of ownership, or by rental, lease, or lending...." (Copyright Law of the United States of America §101)

public domain. Everything that is not protected by copyright and is free for anyone to use.

remaindering. A term for when a book goes out of print and the publisher puts the remaining overstock up for bid.

right of integrity. The author's right that no changes will be made to his or her work without the author's consent.

right of paternity. The author's right to be acknowledged by name on a work.

right to privacy. The right of ordinary people to protect their identity and themselves from unwanted publicity.

right of publicity. A public figure's right to control how his or her image is commercially used.

royalty. A percentage of sales on a work the author receives.

second serial rights. Also known as reprint rights. The nonexclusive right granted to a publication to reprint an article.

subsidiary rights. Additional rights beyond the initial right to publish a book. These can include motion picture/TV rights, novelty rights, serial rights, electronic rights, foreign language rights, audio rights, book club rights, etc.

subsidy publishing. A type of publishing where the author absorbs all costs to produce a book.

term of copyright. The length of time the copyright in a work lasts. Terms vary depending on when the work was created and if it was published or unpublished.

transfer of copyright. "A 'transfer of copyright ownership' is an assignment, mortgage, exclusive license, or any other conveyance, alienation, or hypothecation of a copyright or of any of the exclusive rights comprised in a copyright, whether or not it is limited in time or place of effect, but not including a nonexclusive license." (Copyright Law of the United States of America §101)

unfair competition. The use of a book, lecture, story, poem title, trademark, service mark, identifying material, image, reputation, or other intellectual property for which the original author or owner is well known in order to mislead the public and unfairly benefit from the original author's or owner's reputation or business.

unpublished. A work not made available to the public.

work. Generic term for materials protected by copyright: written works, photographs, maps, illustrations, dramatic presentations, and so forth.

work made for hire, or **work for hire**. "A 'work made for hire' is — (1) a work prepared by an employee within the scope of his or her employment; or (2) a work specially ordered or commissioned for use as a contribution to a collective work, as part of a motion picture or other audiovisual work as a sound recording, as a translation, as a supplementary work, as a compilation, as an instructional text, as a test, as answer material for a test, or as an atlas, if the parties expressly agree in a written instrument signed by them that the work shall be considered a work made for hire...." (Copyright Law of the United States of America §101)

Bibliography

Allen, Moira Anderson. *Writing.com: Creative Internet Strategies to Advance Your Writing Career*. New York: Allworth Press, 2003.

ASMP Professional Business Practices in Photography. 6th ed. New York: Allworth Press, 2001.

Bunnin, Brad and Peter Beren. *The Writer's Legal Companion*. 3d ed. New York: HarperCollins, 1998.

Carmack, Sharon DeBartolo, and Roger D. Joslyn. "Who Owns the Client Report? What We Learned from Being Sued in Federal Court." *Association of Professional Genealogists Quarterly* 16 (June 2001): 137–140.

Copyright Law of the United States of America and Related Laws Contained in Title 17 of the United States Code. Circular 92. Washington, D.C.: U.S. Copyright Office, Library of Congress, June 2003.

Crawford, Tad, and Kay Murray. *The Writer's Legal Guide*. 3d ed. New York: Allworth Press, 2002.

Elias, Stephen, and Richard Stim. *Patent, Copyright & Trademark*. 7th ed. Berkeley, Calif.: Nolo Press, 2004.

Evans, Tonya Marie, and Susan Borden Evans. *Literary Law Guide for Authors*. Philadelphia, Penn.: FYOS Entertainment, 2003.

Fishman, Stephen. *The Copyright Handbook: How to Protect & Use Written Works*. 8th ed. Berkeley, Calif.: Nolo Press, 2005.

———. *The Public Domain: How to Find & Use Copyright-Free Writings, Music, Art & More*. 2d ed. Berkeley, Calif.: Nolo Press, 2004.

Greenwood, Val D. "Copyright and Fair Use." In *Professional Genealogy*, edited by Elizabeth Shown Mills. Baltimore: Genealogical Publishing Co., 2001.

Harper, Timothy. *The ASJA Guide to Freelance Writing*. New York: St. Martin's Press, 2003.

Jassin, Lloyd J., and Steven C. Schechter. *The Copyright Permission and Libel Handbook: A Step-by-Step Guide for Writers, Editors, and Publishers*. New York: John Wiley and Sons, 1998.

Kirsch, Jonathan. *Kirsch's Guide to the Book Contract*. Los Angeles: Acrobat Books, 1999.

———. *Kirsch's Handbook of Publishing Law*. 2d ed. Los Angeles: Acrobat Books, 2005.

Kozak, Ellen M. *Every Writer's Guide to Copyright and Publishing Law*. 3d ed. New York: Henry Holt and Company, 2004.

Ross, Tom, and Marilyn Ross. *The Complete Guide to Self-Publishing*. 4th ed. Cincinnati: Writer's Digest Books, 2002.

Ruberg, Michelle, ed. *Writer's Digest Handbook of Magazine Article Writing*. 2d ed. Cincinnati: Writer's Digest Books, 2005.

Stim, Richard. *Getting Permission: How to License & Clear Copyrighted Materials Online & Off*. 2d ed. Berkeley, Calif.: Nolo Press, 2004.

Taylor, Maureen A., and Sharon DeBartolo Carmack. "Free Art? Not So Fast." *Writer's Digest* (September 2001): 31-33.

Waller, James, ed. *National Writers Union Freelance Writers' Guide*. 2d ed. New York: National Writers Union, 2000.

Wilson, Lee. *The Copyright Guide: A Friendly Handbook to Protecting and Profiting from Copyrights*. 3d ed. New York: Allworth Press, 2003.

Resource Directory

WEB SITES, LINKS, AND ONLINE ARTICLES

10 Big Myths about Copyright Explained
      www.templetons.com/brad/copymyths.html

American Society of Journalists and Authors
      www.asja.org

Authors Guild
      www.authorsguild.org

AuthorsLawyer.com
      www.authorslawyer.com

Copyright Clearance Center
      [not affiliated with the U.S. Copyright Office]
      www.copyright.com

Copyright: Frequently Asked Questions
      www.copyright.gov/help/faq/

Copyright Law of the United States of America
      www.copyright.gov/title17/

Copyright, Photography and the Web
www.chimwasmp.org/photoweb/copyrite.htm

Copyright Table compiled by Cottrill & Associates
www.progenealogists.com/copyright_table.htm

Cyndi's List: Copyright Issues
www.cyndislist.com/copyrite.htm [*sic*]

A History of Copyright in the United States
http://arl.cni.org/info/frn/copy/timeline.html

Ivan Hoffman, Attorney at Law
www.ivanhoffman.com
(There are many articles worth exploring on this site.)

National Writers Union
www.nwu.org

New Rules for Using Public Domain Materials
www.copylaw.com/new_articles/PublicDomain.html

Public Domain Images
www.pdimages.com

Stanford Copyright & Fair Use
http://fairuse.stanford.edu/Copyright_and_Fair_Use_Over
view/

U.S. GenWeb Project: Copyright Information
http://usgenweb.org/volunteers/copyright.shtml

United States Copyright Office
    www.copyright.gov

United States Copyright Office: A Brief Introduction and History
    www.copyright.gov/circs/circ1a.html

When Works Pass into the Public Domain
    www.unc.edu/~unclng/public-d.htm

FOREIGN COPYRIGHT

Australian Copyright Council
    www.copyright.org.au

Copyright Association of Ireland
    www.cai.ie/
    Also see the links at www.cai.ie/new/links/index.htm

Irish Patents Office
    www.patentsoffice.ie/nature-of-copyright.html

UK Patent Office
    www.patent.gov.uk/copy/index.htm

Various International Copyright Treaties
    www.wipo.int/copyright/en/treaties.htm

Still Have Questions?

E-mail your questions for inclusion in the next edition to

sharon@sharoncarmack.com
subject line: Carmack's Copyright Questions

Personal responses cannot be given at this time.

Index